Studies in
Writing & Rhetoric

IN 1980, THE CONFERENCE ON COLLEGE COMPOSITION AND COM-MUNICATION perceived a need for providing publishing opportunities for monographs that were too lengthy for publication in its journal and too short for the typical publication of scholarly books by The National Council of Teachers of English. A series called Studies in Writing and Rhetoric was conceived, and a Publication Committee established.

Monographs to be considered for publication may be speculative, theoretical, historical, or analytical studies; research reports; or other works contributing to a better understanding of writing, including interdisciplinary studies or studies in disciplines related to composing. The SWR series will exclude textbooks, unrevised dissertations, book-length manuscripts, course syllabi, lesson plans, and collections of previously published material.

Any teacher-writer interested in submitting a work for publication in this series should send either a prospectus and sample manuscript or a full manuscript to the NCTE Director of Publications, 1111 Kenyon Road, Urbana, IL 61801. Accompanied by sample manuscript, a prospectus should contain a rationale, a definition of readership within the CCCC constituency, comparison with related publications, an annotated table of contents, an estimate of length in double-spaced 8½ × 11 sheets, and the date by which full manuscript can be expected. Manuscripts should be in the range of 100 to 170 typed manuscript pages.

The works that have been published in this series serve as models for future SWR monographs.

Paul O'Dea
NCTE Director of Publications

The Variables of Composition: Process and Product in a Business Setting

Glenn J Broadhead

and Richard C. Freed

WITH A FOREWORD BY RICHARD C. GEBHARDT

Published for the Conference on College
Composition and Communication

SOUTHERN ILLINOIS UNIVERSITY PRESS
Carbondale and Edwardsville

For Marlis and Julie

Production of works in this series has been partly funded by the Conference on College Composition and Communication of the National Council of Teachers of English.

Printed in the United States of America
Designed by Design for Publishing, Inc., Bob Nance
Production supervised by Kathleen Giencke

89 88 87 86   4 3 2 1

Library of Congress Cataloging in Publication Data

Broadhead, Glenn J., 1942–
   The variables of composition.

   (Studies in writing & rhetoric)
   "Published for the Conference on College Composition
and Communication."
   Bibliography: p.
   1. English language—Rhetoric—Study and teaching.
2. English language—Business English—Study and
teaching (Higher)   I. Freed, Richard C., 1946–
II. Title.   III. Series.
PE1479.B87B76   1986   808'.066651'07   85–14239
ISBN 0–8093–1262–X

Contents

Foreword

Richard C. Gebhardt

OVER THE PAST FEW YEARS, OUR PROFESSION HAS LEARNED MUCH about the processes, strategies, and motives at work in some writing—in "academic, belletristic or literary writing," as Glenn J Broadhead and Richard C. Freed point out. We know far less about the practices and processes of writing in business settings, even though this is where much of all writing takes place and where many of our students will work as writers. *The Variables of Composition* helps fill this gap by describing the writing practices, especially the revision strategies, of professional business writers. Recent studies in academic settings (for instance, revision research by Nancy Sommers and by Lester Faigley and Stephen Witte) describe effective writing as a nonlinear and recursive process in which revision is pervasive and not at all a separate, final stage. Working out of the context of this research but within a business environment, Broadhead and Freed arrive at a somewhat different conclusion. Revision, their research suggests, plays a central role in writing, though effective writing can be quite staged and linear, depending on the writer and circumstances of the writing.

As background to this book, Broadhead and Freed studied the writers and writing circumstances of an international management consulting firm for over two years, focusing on "Baker" and "Franklin," two successful consultants who use highly staged strategies in the proposal writing on which they spend much of their professional time. Broadhead and Freed studied hand-written changes on typed drafts, subjected drafts to computer analysis, and interviewed Baker and Franklin about their approaches to writing. Reporting on their research in this volume, Broadhead and Freed offer useful insights into the realities of high-stakes business writing and also expand our understanding of the processes of composition.

Broadhead and Freed describe a writing environment that is quite structured and pressured. The firm mandates the format, procedures, and lines of argument for proposals, assigning specific writing tasks for which deadlines are usually short. By specializing in proposals for a given industry or purpose, consultants develop strong factual backgrounds and rhetorical repertoires on which to draw when they receive an assignment. The consultants are likely to do their writing by hand on airplanes and in hotel rooms, but a professional word-processing department is available to produce clean drafts for them. Such things influence the way Franklin and Baker write: reducing the need for exploration or incubation, letting them use stock sections and "boiler-plate" to speed drafting, and eliminating much of the need for conceptual or organizational revision. And the rigid segmentation of their proposals (problem, methods, implementation) means segmentation in their writing, since revision of one section does little to advance thinking on the next section. Given such a writing situation, it is not surprising to find, as Broadhead and Freed do, effective written products resulting from staged and apparently linear writing strategies. As they observed in one of Franklin's proposals, "he knows what line of thought he will take, he writes it down, he knocks some of the rough places off, and he sends the proposal to the client."

This study of effective staged writing in business emphasizes how widely writing can vary from person to person, from writing environment to writing environment. If asked "to write about their summer vacation or to write a sonnet," the authors observe, Franklin and Baker "might well display a decidedly nonlinear process of composing; but if their Firm's president asked them to develop a proposal for Company X, their composing process . . . would probably be decidedly linear." Broadhead and Freed also suggest by their analysis of Franklin's and Baker's revision strategies that even *apparently* linear writing may "exhibit the multiplicity and simultaneity of rhetorical and linguistic concerns associated with recursiveness."

In the course of their research, Broadhead and Freed analyzed seven variables of revision: Impetus, Item, Process, Norm, Affective Impact, Orientation, and Goal. *The Variables of Composition* describes these variables in detail and offers researchers a methodology with which to investigate how the variables interact in specific writing strategies, whether linear or recursive. This book also suggests how teachers might make use of the variables of revision to help students learn writing strategies with which to work successfully in business settings.

Acknowledgments

Parts of this study were supported by the Iowa State University English Department, the ISU Graduate College, and the ISU Science and Humanities Research Institute. We particularly wish to thank Professor Frank E. Haggard for his assistance in finding time and funds for the project. We are also grateful for the patient expertise provided by Dr. James Hoekstra of the ISU Computation Center. Finally, we wish to thank the two management consultants identified in the study as Baker and Franklin for their insights and for the extra hours after work which they generously volunteered for our study.

Introduction

In the decade and a half since the appearance of Janet Emig's pioneering study *The Composing Processes of Twelfth Graders* (1971), researchers such as Donald Murray (1978), Sondra Perl (1979), Lillian Bridwell (1980), Linda Flower and John R. Hayes (1980a, 1980b), Nancy Sommers (1980), and Ann Matsuhashi (1981) have shown that many questions need answering as we begin to examine composing processes. To understand how individual writers compose documents, for example, we need to know why and how they generate text, what kinds of changes they make, how they make them, and why they make them. We need to know if they move from "writer-based" to "reader-based" prose in successive drafts. We need to know if their processes are linear or recursive. In particular, we need to know how their revising is related to other phases of their composing processes.

But understanding their writing processes in single documents may be insufficient. Do they generate and revise text similarly for similar documents? Do they use the same or a different strategy for different kinds of discourse? Are their methods similar to or different from those of other writers in similar or different circumstances? How are they influenced by textual cues, by education and training, by occupation, by years or status in a given field, by organizational or disciplinary rules or traditions?

The number and complexity of these primary questions raise a new set of questions about methods. For example, when we gather data, should we assume that writers compose differently in college writing classes or in controlled experiments than they do in "real-life" situations? How might conclusions based on one kind of data (for example, familiar essays) be generalized or compared to findings about other kinds (for example, proposals, reports, personal letters, short stories, requests for bids)? Furthermore, as we attempt to answer any or all of these questions, how might we ensure the validity and reliability of our data and our conclusions. Should we use protocol analysis? Interviews? Computer-assisted statistical analyses? Ethnographic comparisons? Case studies? Some combination of these?

These questions are challenging to researchers both in number and in scope. Perhaps the most helpful recent attempt to address many of these issues is Faigley and Witte's "Analyzing Revision" (1981), which describes the limitations of methods used by previous studies of this subject, presents a new taxonomy of revision, and applies that taxonomy to revisions by college students and professional writers in a controlled experiment. Yet even Faigley and Witte note two important limitations of their study and of previous analyses of revision: first, the "artificiality of the writing situation" (411); second, a lack of consideration of "the most important question: what causes writers to revise?" (412). They conclude that "what we need now are more observational studies of writers revising in nonexperimental situations. . . . We need studies that employ more than one methodology" (412).

In addition to these concerns about methods, there is also concern about the focus of much recent research. Since Emig's study, a wealth of information has been generated by process-oriented research; but according to Judith A. Langer (1984), process studies may be "approaching a theoretical dead end" (118). The recent focus on writing processes "was conditioned by a rejection of the earlier preoccupation with product" (117). But "the separation of process and product," Langer cautions, "is beginning to reemerge as the unnatural dualism that our past might suggest it would inevitably become. Indeed, when reading, writing, or spoken language are separated from the ends they serve, we lose the essence of the process itself. Process does not consist of isolated behaviors that operate willy-nilly, but of purposeful activities that lead toward some end for the person who has chosen to engage in them" (118). Langer's concern stems from researchers' current understanding that writing is written within and for discourse communities, societies whose cultural requirements—and subdisciplines whose values, traditions, and beliefs—condition the writer's own values and influence both the process of composition and the products issuing from that process.

This brings us to a final area of concern: the kinds of writers that researchers have selected for study. Few studies have investigated the discourse community that, along with government, probably produces more writing than any other: writers in business and industry. As recently as 1977, Joseph M. Williams could say that "we know next to nothing about the way individuals judge the quality of writing in places like Sears and General Motors and Quaker Oats. . . . Virtually no such research exists" (9). Despite the excellent work of Odell and Goswami (1982) and others since then, our knowledge is not much greater. We still know next to nothing about the composing and revising processes of writers in business and industry. We still know next to nothing about how composing processes are affected by organizational traditions and practices, or about how writing functions politically within and is affected politically by the organization itself. In short, scholars and teachers have little idea how current theories of composition apply to writing in the business world, where corporate executives and technicians regularly interact through written documents.

There are several reasons for the dearth of research in this area. First and foremost, of course, writing researchers do not often have the opportunity to live within an organization long enough to examine how writing is produced. Second, researchers rarely have access to the written products of business writers, and more rarely still do they have the chance to examine all the drafts such writers use in composing their documents. Third, even when researchers can obtain documents to study, they might not have access to the authors themselves to conduct follow-up interviews. Finally, even when researchers have access to both writers and their documents, they might not have systematic and reliable methods for analyzing and describing their data—partly because most existing methods depend upon "artificial" or controlled situations that can alter the processes being studied, and partly because a number of measures of quantifiable aspects of style are necessary for a full description of the products resulting from the revising process.

Yet for the adequate instruction of our students—many of whom will be writing proposals and reports in the business environment—

it is essential that we understand how that environment operates, how writers compose and revise in (and in response to) that environment, and how those writers' documents can best be analyzed. Our purpose in the present study is therefore threefold. First, we seek to extend the analysis of revision into a "real-world" context by examining the revising practices of proposal writers in a management-consulting firm—a company in which written proposals often determine whether the firm's services will be retained or rejected, and hence whether the writer's career will flourish or wither. Second, we seek to describe writers' motives and intentions in generating and revising a text, so that the pedagogy of composing and revising may rest on a firmer foundation. Third, we attempt to achieve a balanced perspective by examining the ends as well as the means of composing—that is, by focusing on the interplay of product and process.

To address these purposes, our study is organized into four chapters and a conclusion. Chapter 1 describes our seven-variable taxonomy for analyzing the composing process—particularly revision. Where necessary, we briefly discuss the problems with previous research taxonomies that led to our formulation of a new one. Chapter 2 describes our methods of collecting, analyzing, and measuring data. Chapter 3 begins to apply the taxonomy by describing the institutional procedures, values, and constraints characteristic of the "real-world" environment that we selected for study: a large management-consulting firm. Chapter 4 analyzes and compares in detail how two management consultants composed proposals within the framework described in chapter 3. Along the way, we present further methodological and theoretical explanations of our approach, since many of these comments become meaningful only in light of what we observed. Chapter 4 focuses on the patterns of rhetorical choices made by the two writers as they composed four proposals apiece; more specifically, it describes the how and why of what they did and identifies the varying factors that had the dominant impact in each proposal. Finally, the conclusion describes some strengths and limitations of our approach, and also outlines possible areas of future research as well as potential applications of our findings to composition pedagogy.

1

The Variables of Composition

IN THEIR 1981 ARTICLE "ANALYZING REVISION," LESTER FAIGLEY and Stephen Witte introduced a taxonomy of writing processes and textual features that a writer could manipulate while revising (or, by extension, while generating) text. Their taxonomy is based on two features of discourse isolated by text linguistics: first, information, or content; second, the organization of that information into two levels of generalization or logical structure: the "macrostructure," consisting of the most general level of propositions, and the "micro-structure," consisting of the most specific level of propositions. Actually, text linguists such as Teun van Dijk (1980) and Edward J. Crothers (1979) distinguish many levels of generalization or propositional content, but Faigley and Witte appear to reserve the term "macrostructure" for the most general level, treating all lower levels as "microstructure," including some that might be very general relative to the most specific level. Recently, Witte (1983) has moved away from an emphasis on macrostructure to an analysis of "topical structure," another concept borrowed from text linguistics, and one which similarly focuses on the amount of information and the levels of generalization.

For our study of writing in a business setting, however, a focus on macrostructure or the amount of information in a text would draw us away from one of the main things we wanted to examine: writers' reasons for expressing ideas one way rather than another. Besides presenting difficulties of application due to some ambiguous terminology (Broadhead and Freed, forthcoming), the Faigley-Witte taxonomy would make it difficult to see relationships between the revising process and other phases of composing (for example, the stage of generating a text). Their taxonomy would also make it difficult to see how these processes are influenced by the writer's task, audience, and organizational environment. Therefore, we have developed a new method of analysis based on seven "variables" of composition. The method is similar to some aspects of the Faigley-Witte taxonomy, but it allows quantifiable objective processes to be linked to equally quantifiable interpretations of purpose and motive.

As applied to a writer's *revisions*, the seven variables take the form of the following seven questions:

Variable	Question
1. Impetus	Is the change voluntary or nonvoluntary?
2. Item	What is changed?
3. Process	How is the change made?
4. Norm	What prompts the change?
5. Affective Impact	Is the affective impact low or high?
6. Orientation	What is the rhetorical focus?
7. Goal	What is the rhetorical aim?

In the remainder of this chapter, we will briefly define these variables (along with their subcategories) as they apply to the revising process. In chapters 3 and 4, we will show how the variables apply to overall composing processes in the management-consulting firm mentioned earlier and in eight proposals written by two of its management consultants. A summary of the first six variables is presented in Appendix A.1.

Impetus: Is the Change Voluntary or Nonvoluntary?

We first determine whether a revision is undertaken for its own sake (hence "voluntary") or whether it is necessitated by a previous change or an outside force (hence "nonvoluntary"). For example, when one of our writers reviewed the phrase "the study by Principals of our firm who have participated in similar studies," he decided to change "Principals" to "a senior professional." As a result of this voluntary change, he had to make the nonvoluntary change of "have participated" to "has participated" in order to match the verb with its new antecedent noun.

While most nonvoluntary changes consist of such linguistically required alterations, another important subclass consists of logically required changes to signals of cohesion in lists. For example, a writer might first state that there are ten steps in a process, and then signal the discussion of each step with a numerical heading (1 through 10). If the writer later decides that another step occurs between the original steps 5 and 6, then this voluntary insertion of information must be accompanied by a nonvoluntary renumbering of original steps 6 through 10 to 7 through 11. If a nonvoluntary change is required either by grammar or by logic, we call it "involuntary."

Another subclass of nonvoluntary revisions consists of changes to repair typographic errors (especially those made by someone other than the author, such as a word-processing operator). On the one hand, writers repair typos because they want to, so typographic repairs might be considered voluntary. On the other hand, a decision to change the typo "assits" to "assist" seems qualitatively quite different from a decision to change "assist" to "help." The former involves no change to the text that the writer conceived and produced (though it could alter the way a reader might interpret the text); but the latter change does alter the writer's concept, however slightly. For this reason, we treat changes to repair typos as nonvoluntary revisions, and we refer to them as "typographic" revisions.

A third subclass of nonvoluntary changes consists of those made by editors, second authors, or institutional superiors (as when the company president makes or asks for a change in a division manager's report). We call these "second-author" revisions.

The distinction between voluntary and nonvoluntary changes has not been made in many previous studies of revision (for example, Bridwell, Sommers, Faigley and Witte), no doubt because those studies have tended to focus more on *what* changes writers made rather than on *why* the writers made them. In analyses concerned with purpose and motive, however, the distinction can be crucial. For example, a highly skilled writer might produce an error-free text, and then make thirty revisions: ten substantive changes, all voluntary, and each requiring two minor, nonvoluntary adjustments of usage and grammar undertaken only to accompany the ten substantive changes. A relatively unskilled writer, however, might produce an error-ridden text, and thus might also make thirty revisions, all voluntary, with perhaps ten devoted to trifling substantive changes (none of which require concommitant adjustments to the text) and twenty devoted to usage and grammar changes necessary to bring the text up to minimal conformance with standard English. Without the voluntary/nonvoluntary distinction, a quantitative analysis of these two writers' revisions would show only that both made ten substantive changes and twenty changes in usage and grammar—a quantitative similarity suggesting the very misleading conclusion that they both revise the same things the same way.

Item: What Is Changed?

The kinds of linguistic and textual elements or "items" that can be manipulated to make a revision may be ranged into a hierarchy:

Chapter
First-level heading group (that is, a group of paragraphs set off by a heading)
Second-level heading group (that is, a section within a first-level heading group)
Third-level heading group
Paragraph group
Paragraph
Sentence group (a string of related sentences within a paragraph)
Sentence
T-unit (that is, an independent clause plus any dependent structures that modify it)
Macrosyntactic structure (for example, an independent clause, a nonrestrictive relative or subordinate clause, an appositive, a prepositional phrase set off by punctuation)
Bound phrase within a macrosyntactic structure
Word
Alphanumeric character or subword (for example, -ed, -ing, pre-, a, b, c, d, 1, 2, 3)
Punctuation mark

The item variable presents a problem for quantified analysis of revisions. For example, if a word is inserted or deleted, then the item changed is quite clearly a word; but if a word is replaced by a phrase, should the revision be classified as a change of a word or a change of a phrase? Our response to this question is to preserve both perspectives. If something other than a simple insertion or deletion is involved, we record both the "old" item and the "new" one.

Process: How Is the Change Made?

As our discussion of items has suggested, a revision can be accomplished not only by addition or deletion of material but also by four other processes, previously identified by Faigley and Witte and others. To label these processes, however, we prefer to use the simpler terminology employed by many word-processing programs, such as the WYLBUR interactive system: insert (corresponding to Faigley and Witte's add), delete (delete), replace (substitute), move (permutate), split (distribute), and join (consolidate). (The WYLBUR system is fully described by the WYLBUR/370 Reference Manual, copyright 1975, 1977, published by Stanford University.)

Although these terms are more familiar, they share the same potential for ambiguity, since replacements, moves, splits, and joins can be treated as combinations of the two primary processes of insertion and deletion. Physically, for example, writers may "replace" a word with two actions: first, scratching out or deleting the old word; second, writing in or inserting a new word in its place. Similarly, writers may split a paragraph by inserting blank spaces; they may join two sentences (most simply) by deleting the first one's period, inserting a semicolon, deleting the second sentence's initial upper-case letter, and inserting a lower-case letter; and they may move material by deleting it in one place and inserting it elsewhere.

But while insertions and deletions appear to be fundamental to the physical acts involved in making pencil-and-paper revisions, they do not necessarily occur in the physical act of making a change on some word processors. On some computer software, for example, one may physically replace a word through two acts (first "erasing" the old word, then typing in a new one) or through one (in effect, typing the new word over the old one). Indeed, whether the physical change involves two actions or one, only one mental act would appear to be required, since we may conceive of only one command ("replace x with y") rather than two ("delete x; insert y"). Thus, what is true of the physical act of making a revision with pencil on paper (scratching out one word and writing in another) may not be true of the mental act of conceiving of a revision (replacing one word with another).

This distinction at first seems trivial, but it has an important bearing on the quantification of the revisions made in a text. For example, if a writer inserts one paragraph containing ten sentences made up of two hundred words composed of three thousand alphabetical characters and punctuation marks, has there been one change, ten changes, two hundred changes, or three thousand changes? We call this the "moments of revision" problem, which arises because several physical changes might be prompted by only one mental act, one unit of time when the writer decides to make a change in the text (for example, "I need to develop this generalization in this part of my report").

It was this problem which created a need for the hierarchy of items mentioned earlier, ranging from punctuation marks up to heading groups. By recording not only the process but also the item involved in a revision (and also the "range" of the item in terms of the number of macrosyntactic structures that comprise it), we can preserve the conceptual sense of "one revision," but we can also distinguish between small and large changes to the text. For example, when a writer appears in one moment of revision to insert three sentences (each consisting of two macrosyntactic structures) as a new paragraph, we record the change as the insertion of a paragraph with a range of six structures.

Besides the moment-of-revision problem, a final important point about the processes used in revising is that the relationship between items and processes is not symmetrical. That is, some items can be altered by all six processes, but others cannot. A paragraph, for example, can be inserted, deleted, replaced, split, joined to another paragraph, or moved to another part of the text. But a punctuation mark cannot be split.

Norm: What Prompts the Change?

As writers create a text, they are guided by at least five norms: cultural, institutional, generic, personal, and situational. These norms influence both the written product and, in a broader application, the writer's behavior while thinking and composing.

Cultural Norms

In their narrow application to the text, cultural norms govern choices to make the text adhere to a culture's idea of good behavior and good communication in a written document. They are common to writers and readers within a given language or (more commonly) within a recognizable body of language users within a culture. These norms are prescribed by handbooks, textbooks, dictionaries, and the like or are implied by the culture's assumptions about the purposes and values of language and communication.

For example, speech-act theorists such as Austin (1975), Searle (1969), and Grice (1975) postulate some culturally mandated "rules" which people observe in their everyday speech and presumably generalize to their everyday writing. In Grice's view, logical leaps (implications) are possible in conversation because the participants observe culturally sanctioned rules such as "make your contribution as informative as is required for the current purposes of the exchange"; "try to make your contribution one that is true"; "be relevant"; "be orderly"; and (touchingly) "avoid unnecessary prolixity." Other analysts of discourse, such as Donald Allen and Rebecca Guy (1978), emphasize social interaction, such as "bonding" (creating a sense of group identity), "bridging" (establishing common knowledge or attitudes), and "anchoring" (giving some overt if subtle sign that one is an active participant in a "dyad" or a larger group). Like the speech-act "rules," these practices are based on broad, cultural, normative principles (for example, conversers develop "a common consciousness in which each participant comes to see the viewpoint of the other and to take in fully what the other is saying" [p. 102]). Though Allen and Guy's views appear to be colored by the social dogma of, say, Mr. Rogers, their claim that cultural norms of behavior are implicit in oral communication is well taken; and like other researchers, we have extended this claim to written as well as spoken communication.

In their broader application to the writing process, cultural attributes such as age, sex, power, education, skills, prestige, ethnic background, and available resources (such as time and money) affect each writer's performance. That is, while social values such as accuracy, thoroughness, relevance, coherence, and consistency are manifested in a text, culturally mandated procedures and strategies are manifested in the manner in which the text is produced. For example, the general strategy of analyzing, planning, performing, and polishing is applicable not only to composition but also to sports, music, and business affairs.

Institutional Norms

Institutional norms govern rhetorical decisions designed to make a text adhere to accepted practices within a company, profession, discipline, or the like, such as the General Motors Research Institute, the Government Printing Office, the Modern Language Association, the American Psychological Association, the Acme Insurance Company, or Professor Smith's freshman composition class. Examples of institutional norms as applied to texts would be documentation practices (such as APA or MLA), in-house style or format guides, group or disciplinary injunctions such as "do not use the first person," and so forth. These norms, however, need not be formalized in written documents; they can also result from tradition or practice.

In their broader application to the writing process, these institutional norms reflect a writer's overall environment for thinking, composing, and revising. For example, many writers have relatively few institutional constraints: they compose when they please, using whatever means they please (for example, pencil and paper, typewriter, word processor), and they revise or not as often as they please. In contrast, people who write for newspapers, magazines, or businesses are severely constrained in regard to the amount of time available for writing and revising, the means of writing and revising, and the determination of whether revising (of whatever scope or focus) will take place or not.

Generic Norms

Generic norms are those imposed by a particular genre of writing, such as a proposal, a familiar essay, a request for bids, a personal letter to a friend or relative, and the like. As applied to texts, these norms establish conventions of arrangement, argumentation, and physical format, such as the six-part report on empirical research (abstract, introduction, method, results, discussion, conclusion) or the variable-part "technical report" described by Mathes and Stevenson (1976) (for example, cover letter, foreword, summary, introduction, body, conclusions/recommendations). These norms also regulate vocabulary and other elements of style.

Generic norms affect the writing process as well. As an extreme example, a personal letter is generally unrestricted in subject matter, unplanned, unconventionally organized (relatively speaking), and unrevised; typically, it has only one author. But a scientific report generally requires some variation of the "problem/need/solution" line of thought, often in the highly conventional, compartmentalized format of introduction, methods, results, discussion, and conclusion. Because its line of thought and its compartmentalization are so different from those of a personal letter, it is typically composed differently, with a later section (for example, "method") perhaps being written before an earlier one (for example, "introduction"), with several stages of revision taking place, or with several authors contributing different sections or revising each other's work.

Personal Norms

Personal norms are the linguistic or rhetorical preferences of a given writer. Examples as applied to the text might be a writer's characteristic use of wit or euphony, or a preference for "sincerely" rather than "yours truly."

As applied to behavior or process, personal norms can affect the way a particular writer composes and revises. For example, one writer might hoard time to write a letter at one sitting, while another might write a letter in stages over several days. One writer might go through an elaborate "nesting" ritual before composing, while another might compose on the back of an envelope while riding the bus home. One writer might write half a word, erase it, replace it, and continue on, while another might never revise until at least a paragraph has been generated. Personal norms may have even more far-reaching influences on the writing process, as our discussion of two writers will show in chapter 4.

Situational Norms

Situational norms guide writers' decisions about adapting their tone, style, format, selection of content, level of technicality, and so forth, to achieve their own purposes and meet their readers' needs in a specific rhetorical situation. Thus, these norms involve the intended readers' supposed values, the nature of the subject or issues being discussed, and the demands of the rhetorical task.

The writing situation, of course, may also affect the manner in which the document is composed. For example, a college student's letter to Mom and Dad to request $20 might be dashed off without much planning or revising, but a letter to a scholarship fund to request $2000 might be well thought out beforehand and rigorously worked over.

All of these norms—cultural, institutional, generic, personal, and situational—may be thought of as allegorized readers. That is, a writer has not one reader over his shoulder, but five—each corresponding to one of the norms. These readers often have different demands that must be satisfied by different rhetorical strategies. Sometimes those demands conflict, and one may override another. For example, in his first draft, one writer labeled a section of the proposal with the generic heading "Approach." Later, he replaced that heading with the heading that was conventional within his firm: "Plan of Attack." That heading might in turn have been replaced by one addressed to the situational reader, such as "How We Will Proceed," a common-language version appropriate to the informal, personal relationship between the writer and the reader.

And if norms can conflict, they can also merge. In fact, it may be that skilled writers more successfully resolve conflicts between norms by more successfully creating (and revising for) a hypothetical "target" reader in whom the norms are fused into a single point of view or "personality," with clear relationships and patterns of dominance between the respective norms.

Affective Impact: Is the Affective Impact Low or High?

In addition to impetus, item, process, and norm, we further differentiate revisions by whether they have low or high affective impact on the reader. Low-affect changes generally address matters of cohesion, usage, and the cognitive relationship between the reader and the discourse—assuming that nothing in the rhetorical situation invests these elements with high affective value, such as a reader known to be pathologically enraged by an errant pronoun reference, a comma splice, or something else that might not stir a normal reader's passions. For example, a medical writer who in a first draft has mentioned a relatively uncommon disease might later insert a passage describing its symptoms in greater detail so that doctors could understand how to recognize it. Or a pronoun reference might be clarified in order to smooth out the text's line of thought. Such changes would be low in affect. High-affect changes, on the other hand, address social relationships between the reader and the writer; for example, the medical writer might think that the added detail could be considered condescending, and might therefore add the palliative qualification "As you are well aware . . ." High-affect changes might also address the reader's feelings about the subject of the discourse. For example, in a pamphlet for lay readers, a first-draft mention of a disease might be revised with an inserted passage describing its symptoms in gory detail so that readers would definitely want to avoid contracting it.

Orientation: What Is the Rhetorical Focus?

As our discussion of affective impact has implied, a revision may be oriented to one or more of four factors: toward ideas (that is, to the amount of information in a text, to the order of ideas, or to logical, topical, or rhetorical relationships between ideas), toward cohesion, toward style, or toward usage. Depending upon one's perspective, all four factors might or might not be part of the text's meaning.

In general, the first of these orientations involves meaning as *dualistic* theories of style construe it—that is, as involving the referential sense (denotation) and the logical relationships (argument) of the discourse, respectively, with changes in referential meaning being produced mainly by insertions, deletions, and replacements, and with changes in logical meaning being produced partly by the same three processes and partly by moves, splits, and joins.

The latter three orientations deal with aspects of discourse that *monistic* theories of style construe as involving meaning. Cohesion, for example, involves "text-oriented" meaning, or the meaning-creating consistencies of language that operate within a particular text (as described by M. A. K. Halliday's three-part "Notes on Transitivity," 1967, 1968). Similarly, revisions oriented to usage or style involve the social meaning or ethos implied by the sociolinguistic habits and preferences evident in the text.

Orientation toward Ideas

In our treatment of the orientation toward ideas, we depart radically from the Faigley-Witte taxonomy for several reasons. First, the macrostructure/microstructure distinction fails to account for some rhetorically significant revisions. For example, a text might be increased to twice its original size by developing an idea in greater detail, yet the text's macrostructure would be unaltered. Furthermore, a definition of "macrostructure" that is "based on whether new information is brought to the text or old information is deleted," as Faigley and Witte emphatically claim their taxonomy to be, cannot account for major rearrangements of the content into a new line of thought, since by definition material that is moved is neither added nor deleted. Second, the analysis of a text's macrostructure is impractical, since the method of systematic deletion (as propounded by Crothers and by van Dijk) is too time-consuming, given the amount of attention that we devote to other features. Third, because we examine rough and transitional drafts, relationships between ideas cannot always be summarized reliably, since strictly speaking a line of thought (that is, a connection between two ideas or claims) might not even exist in the first or even a later draft; for, even though two juxtaposed sentences might comprise a single paragraph, the connection between the two ideas might be difficult if not impossible to infer. Fourth, since we categorize each revision according to a hierarchy of items (along with its range in terms of macrosyntactic structures), the macrostructure/microstructure distinction is unnecessary. For, if a change in the macrostructure were to occur (at least in texts longer than a couple of hundred words), it would surely involve the insertion of a sentence at the very least. And if the macrostructure change were important enough to have a rhetorical impact on the text, as in the addition of a major topic of discussion, such an addition would surely take the form of an inserted paragraph, paragraph group, or heading group. These insertions are easily classified as one of the "items" previously mentioned. Fifth, and finally, by eliminating the macrostructure/microstructure distinction as a basic category of analysis, we allow for the possibility of comparing revisions in texts of very disparate sizes. For example, take the case of a book's chapter that could be separately published as a self-contained text. A writer might alter the macrostructure of the chapter text without altering the macrostructure of the book. Thus, if we were to try to compare the book writer's revisions with those of the chapter writer, the meanings of the term "macrostructure" would be so different that comparison would be impossible: nothing in the chapter could be construed as a macrostructure change, even though the summary of the chapter might be substantially altered. Conversely, it is much more meaningful to compare insertions, deletions, replacements, joins, splits, and moves of sentences, paragraphs, and the like; for, while these units vary from writer to writer, we further define them by their size (in number of structures), and can thus determine whether our comparisons are reasonable. That is, we can sensibly compare a writer whose paragraphs average four structures in size with a writer whose paragraphs average twelve structures in size, since we can quantify the difference. Thus, we could compare one writer's twenty-structure paragraph with another writer's twenty-structure heading group. But no such quantifiable measure is available for comparing the macrostructure of one text with that of another.

For a variety of reasons, therefore, we define an orientation toward ideas as a change in information, a change in logical relationships, or a change in the order of ideas. Of these, a change in the informational content of the discourse might include either vocabulary or the level of detail to which statements are developed. Many such changes are very slight. For example, if an original text contains the remark "Jim used a hammer to open the door" and a revision changes that to "Jim used a mallet to open the door," we consider the revision to be a change in information, albeit a slight one. In fact, even if two words have the same extension (refer to the same things), we consider the replacement of one with the other a change in information if the terms' intensions differ, as in replacing the word "equilateral" with the word "equiangular." On the other hand, if the sentence were changed to "Jim opened the door by using a hammer," the informational (referential) content of the sentence would not have changed, even though from a monistic point of view the meaning (emphasis, phenomenological quality) might be different. So far as we are aware, the informational content of discourse may be altered only by inserting, deleting, or replacing (the last of which, as noted above, may be thought of as a deletion followed by an insertion); it is possible, however, that the conjunction of two formerly separate ideas in a text might produce a new, third implication, so we continue to look for instances in which informational content is altered by moves, joins, or splits.

A change oriented toward ideas might also involve such broad factors as the argument, plot, or arrangement of the discourse, including any minor change in the order of ideas that is not prompted by cohesion. That is, even a change in the order of structures in a sentence could be a change in the idea, as in the following sentence and its revision:

> Since Aristotle is human, and since all humans are mortal, Aristotle is mortal.

> Since all humans are mortal, Aristotle is mortal, because Aristotle is human.

It is of course much more likely that such a change would be oriented toward cohesion (for example, to connect this argument with a previous discussion of the mortality of humans), but it is at least theoretically possible that, since English is linear (one word coming after another), very small changes in the order of ideas may be rhetorically significant, as in revising an anticlimactic series ("morning, night, and noon") into climactic order ("morning, noon, and night").

But many changes in the organization of ideas (that is, in the line of thought) involve much larger stretches of discourse, and they are accomplished by moving, splitting, or joining sections of the text that already exist, though some also add new or delete old information. For example, if we treated the syllogism about Aristotle's mortality as a complete text with three main sections (or as a summary of a text with three such sections) and if we further supposed that a new section were added, then we might get the following revised text (or summary of a text):

> Since Aristotle is human, and since all humans are mortal, Aristotle is mortal; *so he ought to buy some life insurance.*

That new remark does not develop a previously existing idea, but instead changes the argument and, in this case, the apparent focus or purpose of the text itself. It no longer has the "superstructure" or "line" of premises and conclusion, but instead constitutes a problem-solution argument.

Orientation toward Cohesion

A revision oriented to cohesion is a change in the signals of relationships between one part of the discourse and another—signals extensively described by Halliday in his three-part "Notes on Transitivity" and by Halliday and Ruqaiya Hasan in *Cohesion in English* (1976). Generally speaking, such revisions involve insertions, as in adding a transitional expression (such as "next" or "for example" or "on the other hand") or a heading. But other processes may also be employed in revisions oriented toward cohesion. For example, a transitional expression might be moved to strengthen the signal of relationship, perhaps by splitting off a bound cohesive tie into a free one (as in changing "After that he went to the police" to "After that, he went to the police") or by moving a free modifier to another position (as in changing "His calls to the police did not receive an answer, therefore" to "Therefore, his calls to the police did not receive an answer"). If a cohesive tie is deleted, however, the motive most often is to condense the text, not to signal relationships. Common concerns in revising for cohesion are listed in Appendix A.2 (where they are subdivided by goal) and in the discussion below of goals 6 through 10.

Orientation toward Style

A revision oriented toward style addresses the verbal economy and grace of the text. Often, this involves joins and splits as the writer rids the text of overlong, difficult-to-read structures. For example, the writer may edit out multiply-embedded bound clauses, needless anticipatory constructions, sentence frames, or awkward middle-position free modifiers. Or deadwood and roundabout phrases may be lopped off or replaced with better ones. Finally, the writer may make changes to make the text *sound* better, as in avoiding inadvertent rhymes, awkward phrasing, or weak repetition of words and phrases. Typical concerns are listed in Appendix A.3, and are further described below in the discussion of goals 11 through 14.

Orientation toward Usage

A revision oriented toward usage addresses the correctness of the text—that is, its conformance with sociolinguistic conventions, such as spelling, idiom, capitalization, grammatical agreement, dangling modifiers, and split infinitives. Typical concerns are listed in Appendix A.4, and are further described in the discussion below of goals 15 through 20.

Relationships among Orientations

Our categories of cohesion, style, and usage reflect our desire to be more systematic about the crosscategorized jumble of concerns appearing in most composition handbooks. By stipulating these categories, we have found it much easier to classify our writers' revisions. However, one family of changes remains particularly difficult to classify: shifts in case, mood, number, person, tense, and voice. Although such linguistic regularities play a significant role in the cohesion of a text, we believe that they are not often revised as if they were aspects of cohesion. Our writers (and probably most persons interested in rhetoric, for that matter) tend to make a verb agree with its antecedent noun not in order to be "clear" but in order to be "correct." That is, there is nothing unclear about the sentence "He don't like it," but there is definitely something incorrect about it (according to the norms of standard written English). For this reason, we treat shifts as matters of usage, not as matters of cohesion. In other words, from our point of view, cohesion involves relationships between ideas, not the minimum linguistic regularities with which an utterance or a text must usually conform.

Furthermore, even with these distinctions being stipulated, it is sometimes difficult to classify a particular change—not because the categories are muddy (as they are in the handbooks), but because a particular change might be made for reasons related to one or more of the categories. For example, a writer might change "This is clear" to "This point is clear" because the cohesion of the text (the clarity of the reference word "this") would be improved by the lexical cohesion supplied by the word "point"; or, assuming that the reference of "This" might be perfectly clear without the lexical boost provided by "point," the writer might still insert "point" out of conformance with the usage rule that a demonstrative pronoun should never be used without a noun immediately following it. Similarly, a stretch of text (a paragraph, a sentence, a structure, or a phrase) might be segmented for several reasons: to clarify the relationship between ideas (as in breaking up an independent clause into a base clause and a free modifier so that the resulting structure echoes the structure of a previous passage); to improve the comprehensibility or readability of the text (as in breaking up an overlong independent clause into a base clause and a free modifier so that the burden on short-term memory is reduced); to conform with a rule of usage (as in obeying a rule to set off the last element in a series with a comma); or to alter emphasis or otherwise change the meaning (as in setting off the last element in a series with a dash so that it receives greater emphasis: "He was a Boy Scout, a choir boy—and a chainsaw murderer").

Naturally, this multiplicity of motives for a change can make categorization difficult. Whenever possible, therefore, we ask writers what they had in mind (or at least what they think they had in mind) when they made a change. In the event that a writer cannot be asked, cannot remember, or just does not answer—that is, when we can gain no entry to the writer's mind—we categorize according to effect rather than intent. But even this leaves a further problem of categorization unsolved. Although the application of a taxonomy leads us to expect "either/or" categories, writers revise by developing and then implementing conscious choices, and the reality of the mind is that a writer's single act of revision could be oriented toward two or even more aspects of discourse. For example, a writer might see that a word is misspelled; but instead of simply correcting the spelling, the writer might replace the word with one whose meaning is slightly different. Thus, the revision would be oriented not toward either usage or idea, but toward both usage and idea. In practice, such instances of multiple orientations appear to be rare; so, for purposes of quantification, we think it convenient (and seldom misleading) to describe any particular revision as being oriented to just one of the three orientations or to one of twenty-six goals (described in the next part of this chapter). The categories are viewed not as mutually exclusive but as hierarchically inclusive in the following order:

idea
cohesion
style
usage

The rationale for this hierarchical ranking is that cohesion exists to show the relationships between ideas; style is subservient to cohesion, since a clear line of thought can be signaled even in wordy sentences, but concise sentences may do nothing to clarify relationships between ideas in different sentences or parts of the text; and usage can be considered a particular type of group style. Correctness is usually less important to communication than the interconnectedness of ideas and the economy, clarity, or appropriateness of expression.

Goal: What Is the Rhetorical Aim?

The contextual and purposive elements of norm, affect, and orientation coalesce into immediate goals of revision. In the case of our proposal writers, we have identified twenty-six such goals (see Appendix A.5), which we will define briefly in this chapter and then illustrate in greater detail as we examine the two writers in chapter 4. For now, we are concerned with what the goals are and how they relate to the variables of orientation, norm, and affect. We will first discuss low-affect goals in each of the four orientations (ideas, cohesion, style, and usage); then we will discuss high-affect goals.

We wish to emphasize that, while other writers might share some or all of these goals, they might also have different ones. In other words, our list of goals is not exhaustive, but includes only those sought by our writers as they composed their particular proposals.

Low-Affect Goals Oriented toward Ideas

Whether they involve information, logical relationships, or rhetorical ordering, low-affect idea-oriented changes reflect five immediate goals, numbered here 1 through 5.

Goal 1: To Be Accurate. This goal involves the writers' voluntary efforts to improve the accuracy of their remarks, including not only the truth of their propositions but also the accuracy of the language used to express such propositions.

Goal 2: To Be Safe. Closely akin to the goal of accurate expression is the goal of safe expression. With this goal in mind, writers usually add qualifying words and phrases. Sometimes, however, they remove or replace assertions (explicit or implicit) whose truth is problematical or whose scope might commit the writers or their companies to perform more than they intend to undertake.

Goal 3: To Be Thorough. In meeting this goal, writers extend the scope of a claim or promise; that is, in terms of textbook rhetoric, they "develop" an idea or introduce a new subtopic. Such changes may be undertaken for logical or rhetorical consistency in the level of detail for comparable ideas, for organizational or personal standards of completeness, or for situational needs (for example, if a technical idea has to be explained more fully for lay readers than for experts). Or they may be undertaken to give special treatment to a particular point.

Goal 4: To Be Relevant. The obverse of being thorough is being relevant (eliminating irrelevant information). These deletions may be prompted by cultural norms (deleting information for symmetrical treatment of similar ideas), by institutional norms (deleting information to achieve a standard length for a particular kind of document), or by situational norms (deleting information to avoid confusing a reader with too many details).

Goal 5: To Be Coherent. Some low-affect, idea-oriented revisions alter the logical or rhetorical structure of the text. These changes involve moves of sentences or larger units of the text. Moves *within* sentences are viewed as being directed toward accuracy of expression (goal 1) or toward cohesion (goals 9 and 11, as described below).

Low-Affect Goals Oriented toward Cohesion

We subdivide the general aim of achieving cohesion into five goals based on the means used to signal the relationship. These goals are here numbered 6 through 10.

Goal 6: To Signal Relationships with a Cohesive Tie. Cohesive ties include adverbs ("however"), prepositional phrases ("in the first place"), and infinitive phrases ("to conclude") that are either bound (not set off by punctuation) or free (set off by punctuation). Other cohesive devices include grammatical articles (function words, such as "a" or "the") and pronouns ("she," "it," "each," "both," "several").

Goal 7: To Signal Relationships with Punctuation. Changes for this goal consist mainly of efforts to punctuate potential free modifiers in order to clarify the structure of ideas. For example, sometimes readers have difficulty knowing when one structure stops and another begins:

When he saw the people he knew the bus had arrived.

In the context of a particular text, the relationship between ideas might be determinable as the sentence stands; but relationships could be signaled more clearly by punctuation, yielding either of the following:

When he saw the people he knew, the bus had arrived.

When he saw the people, he knew the bus had arrived.

Often, such changes do not obviously improve the comprehensibility of a text, but they do improve its readability (that is, they make the parts in the whole easier to perceive), as when the first of the following sentences is altered with a comma to create the more clearly segmented second sentence:

Objectives of separate organizational units are not entirely similar nor are they necessarily compatible in all cases.

Objectives of separate organizational units are not entirely similar, nor are they necessarily compatible in all cases.

Goal 8: To Signal Relationships by Graphic Means. In achieving this goal, writers insert or delete headings, break one paragraph into two or join two into one, and highlight passages by italicizing them, underscoring them, or setting them off with "white space."

Goal 9: To Signal Relationships through Syntax. In achieving this goal, writers alter syntax to show the functional similarity or difference in the ideas expressed in the structures. As Francis Christensen emphasized (Christensen and Christensen, 1978), writers may cast (or recast) ideas into parallel sequences of structures (as in the first sentence below) or into nonparallel sequences (as in the second sentence below) in order to signal similarity or dissimilarity of the ideas in the structures:

Angry over the delay, yet still hopeful that the plane would eventually arrive, she drove to the airport.

When he stands behind the lectern, squat and powerful, his round face breaking into laughter, his listeners both love and believe him.

Goal 10: To Signal Relationships by Lexical Means. Writers link ideas lexically by repetition of a key term, by synonyms, or by frame sentences ("Three precepts must guide our actions"). It is sometimes difficult to distinguish between words inserted for this goal (cohesion by lexical means) and those inserted for goal 1 (accuracy of expression). In such cases, if the inserted word does not clearly link up with a word in an adjoining structure, we classify it as a goal 1 change.

Low-Affect Goals Oriented toward Style

We subdivide a writer's concern with style into four goals, here numbered 11 through 14.

Goal 11: To Be Readable. With this goal in mind, writers make the text easier to read and comprehend by combining, breaking up, or otherwise recasting difficult-to-understand structures. As such, this goal is similar to goal 7, signaling relationships through punctuation. However, goal 11 changes require more drastic adjustments to the text: not just inserting punctuation to signal the relationship between existing (though unpunctuated) structures, but rather recasting an existing structure into a different syntactic or rhetorical pattern. For instance, an overlong single structure may be recast into two or more structures to improve readability:

> Planning the task before we attempt to perform it allows us to save much valuable time.

> By planning the task before we attempt to perform it, we save much valuable time.

Goal 12: To Condense. Writers eliminate wordiness mainly by eliminating redundancy and by avoiding needless nominalization (for example, changing "he brought about a change in the system" to "he changed the system"—assuming that the distinction expressed by the nominalization is not relevant or necessary).

Goal 13: To Avoid Weak Repetition. Many changes are intended to eliminate redundancy or ineffective repetition, including unintentional chimes of affixes (for example, "measuring marketing").

Goal 14: To Sound Good. For this infrequent goal, writers attempt to create euphonious or personally desirable phrasing.

Low-Affect Goals Oriented toward Usage

We subcategorize goals oriented toward usage by the means through which correctness is achieved (goals 15 through 20).

Goal 15: To Spell Correctly. Changes to repair spelling are generally straightforward but are occasionally difficult to distinguish from changes in idea (when a misspelling creates a different meaning than that intended, as in "hare" for "hair"). If meaning is potentially altered, we consider the change to be directed toward goal 1 (accuracy).

Goal 16: To Use Idiomatic or Conventional Phrasing. This includes choices such as those between "different from" and "different than," "further" and "farther," "stood in line" and "stood on line," and "take it there" and "bring it there." It also includes second-language problems such as "combing his hairs."

Goal 17: To Capitalize Letters Correctly. This is not often a goal of voluntary changes by mature writers but is a frequent goal of involuntary changes that accompany goal 11 revisions. For example, if the period separating two sentences is replaced with a semicolon, the first alphabetical letter in the second clause must be changed from upper to lower case.

Goal 18: To Observe Usage. This goal includes attempts to avoid split infinitives, dangling modifiers, improper use of contractions or apostrophes, use of "none" as a plural, and the like.

Goal 19: To Punctuate Correctly. This includes all noncohesive punctuation, such as colons after salutations, periods after abbreviations, semicolons outside of quotation marks, and commas to set off the last element in a series (when the relationship between elements in the series is not obscured by the absence of punctuation).

Goal 20: To Achieve Grammatical Agreement or Conventional Syntax. Many changes are intended to make a verb match up in number or person with a noun, a noun with a noun or pronoun, a pronoun with a pronoun, and the like. Very often, too, a voluntary change requires an involuntary adjustment of a passage in order to achieve conventional syntax. For example, a writer might decide to make an idea-oriented change for accuracy (goal 1), changing the "one" in the following sentence to "two": "One of the members was absent." To do so, the writer would also have to make an involuntary goal 20 revision, changing "was" to "were" for noun-verb agreement. Similarly, as a previous example has shown, a writer might split off part of a clause in order to achieve readability (goal 11):

> Planning the task before we attempt to perform it allows us to save much valuable time.

> By planning the task before we attempt to perform it, we save much valuable time.

In such a case, we would treat the split as a voluntary change, and we would consider the insertion of "By," the insertion of a comma, and the replacement of "allows us to" by "we" to be involuntary goal 20 adjustments to achieve conventional syntax.

High-Affect Goals

Low-affect goals, as we have seen, are oriented toward the idea, toward cohesion, toward style, or toward usage. They are generally prompted by cultural, institutional, generic, or personal norms— though some changes for thoroughness are prompted by a reader's cognitive needs, as are some changes for relevance. But in many cases when situational norms prompt a change, we must shift our perspective to account for a new factor. In a sense, so far as the text is concerned, it is still idea, cohesion, style, or usage that is addressed. But so far as the writer's goals or intentions are concerned, these matters are subsumed by a different, overriding concern. As a result, an entirely different set of categories is necessary for a thorough analysis. In our study, we have discovered revisions motivated by the following six high-affect goals.

Goal 21: To Avoid a Threat. To achieve this goal, writers remove a claim or implication that might threaten the position or well-being of the reader.

Goal 22: To Avoid an Insult. To achieve this goal, writers remove a claim or implication that might ridicule or insult the reader.

Goal 23: To Bond with the Reader. At times, writers seek to establish rapport with a reader. Such changes may consist of a simple, well-placed use of the reader's first name to an overt expression of friendship, or it may involve both ("Dave, I look forward to working with you on this project").

Goal 24: To Build Credit. Achieving this goal involves adding claims or implications—either about the writer or about the writer's firm—that would impress the reader (or that would eliminate self-damaging claims or implications). Many of these revisions deal with the firm's ability to help the client (showing that the firm is ready, willing, and able to do so).

Goal 25: To Create or Feed a Wish. To achieve this goal, writers stress positive results for the reader, or else they create or satisfy a need in the reader. Often, these revisions are prompted by generic requirements to establish a need for change—that is, to confirm the reader's concern about the status quo and hence the belief that consulting assistance is needed. Other changes are intended to "decenter" the text: they move *away* from a focus on the writer's task as a proposal writer or on the firm's task as a consulting source, and they move *toward* a clear concern with the client's own problems. In yet other cases, revisions may simply alter the tone to establish a positive mood, as in changing the abstract linking expression "such a result" to a phrase that clearly expresses the desires of the client: "such a success."

Goal 26: To Stroke the Reader. To achieve this goal, writers add claims or implications that commend or flatter the reader.

According to our analysis, then, seven variables are involved in revising: the impetus of the change (two types), the item changed (eleven or more types), the process used to make the change (six types), the norm that prompts the change (five types), the affective impact of the change (two types), the orientation of the change (four types), and the rhetorical goal of the change (twenty-six types). In other words, if we do not count the goals (which are subsumed under orientation, norm, and affect) or the impetus, any of six processes could be applied to any of eleven kinds of items, with either high or low affect, oriented toward any of four factors, and prompted by any of five norms. As a writer sits down to revise a text, therefore, the number of available things to do is $2 \times 11 \times 6 \times 5 \times 4$, yielding 2640 ways of "making a revision." In actuality, however, fewer than 2640 ways exist, since some of the concatenations of the variables are not possible (for example, one cannot split an alphabetical character or a punctuation mark). Even so, the sheer number of ways that are possible supports the increasingly common claim that revision is a complicated process. In the following chapter, we will describe the methods that we used to observe, analyze, and measure this process in a business context.

2

Methods of Collecting and Analyzing Data

FOR TWO YEARS, ONE OF THE RESEARCHERS AVERAGED ONE DAY per week at a management-consulting firm, where he observed the composing and revising practices among consultants from eight of the firm's United States and Canadian offices. The consultants were asked to provide all the data available about a proposal which they had recently drafted, such as the initiating request for a proposal, documents supplied by the potential client, notes from meetings with the client and with other staff at the organization, and all drafts of the proposal (including copies of previous proposals that might have been "cannibalized" or "boilerplated" in the process of writing the new proposal).

Writers who could supply a complete set of such data were asked to respond to questionnaires about their general writing habits and to write a detailed account of their writing and revising processes for the document to be studied. Other information was subsequently gathered during follow-up interviews.

During this initial survey of the organization, we identified two writers who could supply four complete sets of data (client's request for proposal and other material, if any; notes from staff meetings and interviews; and copies of all drafts of each proposal). We will call these two consultants Baker and Franklin.

In analyzing the data, we attempted to focus equally on the products and processes of revision. This focus seemed appropriate, since our approach (and our data) presupposed definable stages in the writing process—for example, the stage prior to the writing of the first draft, the stage at which the first draft had been generated and a fair copy typed up, the stage at which revisions to the first draft had been completed and a fair copy of the second draft had been typed up, and so on to the stage of a final draft that was signed and sent off to the client. (Important stipulations about our use of the term "draft" are presented in chapter 4 in the section headed "Baker's Process in Proposal Bak-A.")

Thus, instead of having a videotape of a writer revising, we had the equivalent of a slide show. But we believe our approach to the discrete drafts was detailed enough to recover (hypothesize) a good deal of information about the active processes that produced each successive draft. In our approach, each draft was analyzed for static features of style such as sentence structure and cohesion, using the system of analysis described by Broadhead, Berlin, and Broadhead (1982), and also using several specially designed computer programs. Then, each draft was compared with the original and subsequent drafts to reveal the dynamic interplay of the seven variables during the revising sessions that created each draft.

First, the text of each draft was examined from the perspective of "macrosyntax," a level of analysis initiated by Francis Christensen. From this perspective, twenty kinds of macrosyntactic structure may be identified: five kinds of independent clauses and fifteen kinds of "free modifiers" (that is, structures set off from the independent clauses by punctuation), as shown in Appendix B.1, "Macrosyntactic Structures." The fifteen kinds of free modifiers were ranged into seven families, also shown in Appendix B.1. The complete text was entered into a computer file, one macrosyntactic structure at a time. In addition, coded descriptive information about each structure was entered into the computer file. Some of this coded material was entered into a nineteen-character fixed format at the beginning of each line of the file, while other material was embedded within the text itself.

For each structure, the following information related to quantifiable stylistic variables was coded into the computer file line in which the structure appeared.

1. The formal type of the structure, by family and species (again, see Appendix B.1, "Macrosyntactic Structures").

2. The position of free modifiers relative to the independent clause they modified: initial, coming before an independent clause;

middle, coming within an independent clause; and final, coming after an independent clause. These are illustrated in the following examples, in which the structure in the position being illustrated is in italics:

> Initial: "*Since she knew that her clients were interested,* Louise explained the procedure again."

> Middle: "Louise, *since she knew that her clients were interested,* explained the procedure again."

> Final: "Louise explained the procedure again, *since she knew that her clients were interested.*"

In addition, free modifiers in each of these positions might have other free modifiers within them, illustrated as follows:

> Within Initial: "Since she knew that her clients (*Neil and Ruth Thompson*) were interested, she explained the procedure again."

> Within Middle: "Louise, since she knew that her clients (*Neil and Ruth Thompson*) were interested, explained the procedure again."

> Within Final: "Louise explained the procedure again, since she knew that her clients (*Neil and Ruth Thompson*) were interested."

Each of these six positions was assigned a numerical label according to the following scheme:

1 = initial
2 = within initial
3 = within middle
4 = middle
5 = final
6 = within final

In this scheme, the even numbers represent structures calling for pairs of punctuation marks, while the odd numbers usually represent structures calling for only a single punctuation mark. An important exception is the designation "within middle" (position 3), which signifies not only structures that are within a middle-position free modifier (and thus require a pair of punctuation marks) but also those that are within the punctuation that sets off a middle-position free modifier. Thus, the structure "i.e." in the following sentence would be classified as position 3 even though it requires only one punctuation mark:

Her clients (*i.e.*, Neil and Ruth) were interested.

Each structure's position label can be attached to its numerical form (family/species) label, yielding a three-digit label which shows a free modifier's "type" (that is, its combined form-kind and position-kind). The utility of these three-digit labels is discussed later in this section.

3. The punctuation mark (if any) or marks used to set off the structure.

4. An evaluation of the appropriateness or correctness of the punctuation (appropriately punctuated, inappropriately punctuated, unpunctuated).

5. The internal structure of independent clauses (for example, noun/verb, noun/verb/noun, passive voice; see Appendix B.2, "Internal Structure of Independent Clauses").

6. The textual function of free modifiers, whether developmental, transitional, linking, or commentative. If developmental, they provide additional information about the idea expressed in another structure. If transitional, they show the relationship between two or more structures by means of a conventional expression, such as "for example," "first," "on the one hand," or "however." If linking, they show a relationship by means of a nonconventional expression, such as a summary of a previous idea in order to prepare for a new one, as illustrated by the subordinate clause in the following sentence: "After she had finished cleaning the machine, she began to reassemble it." If commentative, they indicate the writer's attitude toward the idea being developed in the text, as in the expressions "alas" or "hopefully."

7. The functional similarity of form between two or more structures in a segment of the discourse. For example, functionally similar information might be expressed within formally similar or "echoing" structures, such as the appositives or "noun clusters" in the

following sentence: "She gave money to her brother (Jim) and to her sister (Meg)." Or an echoing pattern of structures in two sentences might signal a similarity of function: "Lazy, he let the dishes pile up in the sink. Manipulative, he got his roommate to clean them."

8. The beginning and ending of bound ("restrictive") relative clauses within a macrosyntactic structure.

9. The beginning and ending of bound ("restrictive") subordinate clauses within a macrosyntactic structure.

10. Four classes of cohesive ties, based on Halliday and Hasan (additive, sequential, qualificatory, logical).

11. Pronouns, subdivided into personal and impersonal.

12. Parenthesized citations of sources.

13. Parenthesized references to tables, charts, or the like.

14. Words or phrases emphasized by italics or other unusual typeface.

15. Errors in cohesion.

16. Errors in style.

17. Errors in usage.

18. Asides (parenthesized sentences and larger elements).

19. Words, phrases, formulas, and the like that are highlighted by indentation and use of "white space," asterisks, dots, dashes, or other techniques.

The first draft of each proposal was entered into a computer file in the manner just described, with each line in the file consisting of a nineteen-character coded description followed by the text of the structure (with other coded material embedded in it). Once the first draft had been entered, the second draft (and subsequent drafts) could be entered into another file, using the same line numbers for structures repeated in both drafts, and using new decimal line numbers for new structures in a subsequent draft; that is, if a new structure had been inserted in draft two between old structures 20 and 21 of the first draft, the new structure could be entered on line 20.5.

Furthermore, as each repeated or new structure was entered into the second-draft file (or files for subsequent drafts), additional coded symbols were embedded in the text. In this additional coding system, a lower-case letter indicates the type of process used to make a particular revision (i = insert, d = delete, r = replace, j = join, s = split, m = move), while a pair of underscores marks the starting and ending point of each change and a numeral shows the number of the draft in which the revision occurs. For example, drafts one and two of a text in their natural state might look like the following:

After a long day in the forest, the bears were tired and hungry. When they entered their home, consequently, they were mad too.

After a hard day in the woods, with little to show for their efforts, the bears were tired and hungry. When they went inside their home, therefore, they soon became angry as well.

As coded in the computer file, they look like the following examples, in which, for each structure (line), the coded information appears on the left, the line number appears in the middle, and the text appears on the right:

```
p 511 ,ad 1020    After a long day in the forest
  010 . 5 1021    the bears were tired and hungry
s 611 ,ad 1022    When they entered their home
  411 ,at 1023    consequently
  010 . 4 1024    they were mad too

p 511 ,ad 2020    After a 2r_hard_ day in the 2r_woods_
  631 ,ad 2020.5  2i_with little to show for their efforts_
  010 . 5 2021    the bears were tired and hungry
s 611 ,ad 2022    When they 2r_went inside_ their home
  411 ,at 2023    2r_therefore_
  010 . 8 2024    they 2i_soon_ 2r_became angry as well_
```

Once the texts of each draft were coded and entered into a computer file, other computer programs, all designed by James Hoekstra of the Iowa State University Computation Center, counted words as well as the various coded features in these files and calculated over two hundred measures of quantifiable aspects of style. Of these measures, thirty-three are reported in the discussion of the proposals as a whole in chapter 4. In the same chapter, eight of the thirty-three measures are reported for each draft of each proposal. These eight are marked with an asterisk in the following descriptions of the thirty-three measures; and for economy of future reference, abbreviations used for these variables in the tables in Appendix C are indicated in parentheses. Besides explaining what the measures are, we also describe the assumptions that we make about their significance, based on published research and on another study currently in progress. And while we speak here mainly about the significance of these measures in describing the skill or sophistication of a writer, in chapter 4 we will also talk about the significance of these measures in characterizing successive drafts of a text (as they demonstrate greater skill or sophistication).

Category 1. Syntactic Complexity and Variability

*T-Unit Mean.** A T-unit or "terminable unit" (that is, an independent clause plus any dependent structures that modify it) is a measure devised by Kellogg Hunt (1966) to measure one aspect of syntactic complexity in the writing of elementary school children, who frequently neglect to punctuate the juncture between independent clauses. It has since become a standard measure in experimental studies of the effect of sentence-combining instruction (for example, Morenberg, Daiker, and Kerek, 1978), where it is considered to yield more accurate information than the mean for sentence length.

Independent Clause Mean (Ind Cl Mean).* Since both sentences and T-units can be increased or decreased in size by the addition or deletion of free modifiers as well as bound modifiers, the T-unit mean by itself is inadequate as an indicator of linguistic tendencies in mature, skilled writers and texts— a point first raised by Christensen in "The Problem of Defining a Mature Style" (Christensen and Christensen, 1978). A fifty-word T-unit (like a fifty-word sentence) can consist of one structure (an independent clause) or several (an independent clause plus one or more free modifiers). If it consists of one structure, the burden on a reader's short-term memory is relatively great, since the reader must discover or impose the grammatical relationship between words and phrases in order to determine meaning before he or she can store meaning; but if the fifty-word T-unit is segmented into several relatively short structures, the grammatical patterns and hence the meaning are more easily apprehended; consequently, the passage is easier to read and understand. For this reason, the independent clause mean is an important index of linguistic trends in a text when viewed in relation to the T-unit mean (see Broadhead and Berlin, 1982).

Difference Between T-Unit and Independent Clause Means (TU/IC Difference). Because of the distinctions just raised, the difference between T-unit and independent clause means is a useful index of complexity: we assume that the higher the mean TU/IC difference, the greater the segmentation of the text, and hence the greater the readability of the text (see Broadhead, Berlin, and Broadhead, 1982).

Standard Deviation of the T-Unit Mean (T-Unit S.D.). This measure of variability indicates the writer's flexibility: the higher the standard deviation, the more varied the writer's syntactic constructions. We assume that the greater the variety of syntax, the more likely it is that the writer is responding stylistically to the demands of expressing particular and distinct ideas.

Bound Clauses Rate. Another measure of complexity is the rate (per 100 T-units) of *bound* relative and subordinate clauses (that is, those that are not set off by punctuation but are instead used as restrictive adverbial, adjectival, or nominal modifiers). This measure also reflects the readability of the text, since bound clauses increase the difficulty of apprehending grammatical structure—particularly when they are embedded within one another, as in "The man the dog the rat bit chased died."

Length of Largest T-Unit (Largest T-Unit). The *minimum* T-unit length rarely provides much insight into what is occurring in a text since it is almost always a two- or three-word formulaic phrase (for example, "See Figure 12"). But the large end of the range provides useful information since the length of the largest T-unit, we believe, may reflect the writer's verbal daring or indifference: the higher the number, the more likely it is that the writer is either very good (if the T-unit is segmented into several stuctures) or very bad (if there is little or no segmentation of the T-unit); the lower the number, the more likely it is that the writer seeks a conservative level of style, being superior to the horrors of nonsegmented monstrosities, but either unable or unwilling to create long, complicated T-units even when they are necessary or desirable.

Category 2. Syntactic Variety

Number of Kinds of Macrosyntactic Structures (Macro Kinds). This is a direct measure of syntactic variety. For examples of the twenty kinds of macrosyntactic structure, see Appendix B.1.

Initial-Position Free Modifiers as a Percent of All Structures (Pct Init FMs). Initial-position free modifiers are frequently used for cohesion, tying a previous idea to the idea in the upcoming clause or larger structure. But while they correlate highly with the rate of cohesive ties, they are also an index of variety when viewed in the context of the percentage of free modifiers in other positions. Thus, the combined percent of free modifiers in initial, middle, and final position is a good measure of style: we assume that the higher the percent, the greater the sophistication of the writer.

Middle-Position Free Modifiers as a Percent of All Structures (Pct Mid FMs). Middle-position free modifiers are used to develop ideas or to signal connections between ideas; usually, a particular writer will tend to emphasize one use or the other. In this study, however, this measure is viewed primarily as a measure of variety (in the context of percentages of free modifiers in other positions).

Final-Position Free Modifiers as a Percent of All Structures (Pct Final FMs).* As Christensen noted in several of his collected essays (Christensen and Christensen, 1978), many professional writers in magazines such as *The Atlantic* employ a "cummulative" style, in which generalizations expressed in a base clause (the first independent clause in a sentence) are developed in detail in final-position free modifiers. Thus, this subcategory is a measure of the sophistication or professional quality of a writer's prose.

Number of Words in Final-Position Free Modifiers as a Percent of the Total Number of Words (Pct Fin FM Words).* Although the number of final-position free modifiers is usually adequate as an indication of sophistication, the percent of words in such structures yields a little more detailed information and was therefore the measure favored by Christensen. It is included here for purposes of comparison with Christensen's data.

Percent of Free-Modifiers within Other Free Modifiers as a Percent of All Structures (Pct FMs in FMs). As noted in the earlier discussion of free modifiers, this measure is another index of a complicated syntax and therefore (we assume) of relative sophistication.

Number of Types of Internal Structures for Independent Clauses (Clause Types). This is another measure of variety and flexibility, showing the extent to which the writer uses patterns other than the most common one of noun/verb/noun—which in turn is the most common variety of the subject/verb/ object pattern ("Jim drives a truck," as opposed to "Jim drives in town").

Category 3. Linguistic Cohesion

*Cohesive Ties Rate.** The number of cohesive ties per one hundred T-units is a measure of a writer's efforts to connect one segment of text with another by means of formulaic expressions (for example, "thus," "next," "for example"), whether bound or free.

Cohesive Free Modifiers Rate (Cohesive FM Rate). Another measure of connectedness in a text is the rate of cohesive free modifiers per one hundred T-units. This measure includes not only conventional expressions but also text-specific "linking" free modifiers, such as "*Having reviewed Stephen's data,* we can see that several questions remain."

Pronouns Rate. Pronouns are yet another means of cohesion in a text—a simple means often favored by relatively unskilled writers. As with other quantifiable factors, rates for pronouns are expressed as the number per one hundred T-units.

Echoes Rate. In many instances, parallelism of phrases or macro-syntactic stuctures signals connectedness by expressing similar ideas in similar structures. Such parallelism includes not only parallel sequences of free modifiers of the sort termed "coordinate" by Christensen, but also parallel structures that may be a considerable distance from one another in a paragraph or larger stretch of text. For example, the subordinate clause "When she was at work . . ." that begins one paragraph might be echoed at the beginning of a subsequent paragraph by "When she was at home. . ." This technique is favored by more sophisticated writers and usually stands in an inverse relationship to the rate of pronouns and bound cohesive ties.

Non-Comma Punctuation as a Percent of All Punctuation (Pct Non-Commas). Since punctuation is a means of signaling connections between ideas, the amount of non-comma punctuation (semicolons, colons, dashes, and parentheses) is another measure of cohesion. But as preliminary results from a study (in progress) of seventy writers in literary and engineering journals suggest, this measure is ambiguous in and of itself, since the non-commas might consist of roughly equal proportions of the four marks (characteristic of highly sophisticated writers), large proportions of semicolons (favored by fairly sophisticated writers), or nearly exclusive reliance on colons and parentheses (favored by relatively unsophisticated writers).

Unpunctuated Macrosyntactic Structures (Pct Unpunctuated). While free modifiers may occur in a text, they may or may not be punctuated as such. By failing to signal the junctures between structures with punctuation, a writer ignores an opportunity for improving the connectedness of a text. We assume that, the more often readers must determine grammatical junctures unaided by punctuation, the more difficult the text is to read and comprehend.

Cohesion Error Rate. In addition to the positive measures already described, we examined the proposals for instances in which necessary or desirable signals of relationships were missing or inadequate. For a list of cohesion errors, see Appendix A.2. The measure is expressed as the rate of such errors per one hundred T-units.

Category 4. Graphic Cohesion

*Headings Rate.** Headings constitute a cohesive device that is seldom used in belletristic writing or fiction but is of course very frequent in business and technical writing. In general, writers who use sophisticated cohesive devices such as echoes tend to write longer paragraphs with fewer headings; writers who are relatively unsophisticated tend to rely on pronouns (as noted earlier) and on a relatively higher number of headings (see Broadhead, Berlin, and Broadhead, 1982).

Highlights Rate. Highlighting is the practice of setting off phrases or words in a sentence by indentation and other means (such as "dots," "dashes," or "bullets"). It is used by all writers as a means of emphasis and by less skilled writers as a means of clarity (that is, as a graphic way of breaking up an overlong structure for readability). Highlighting practices in the management-consulting firm that we observed are described more fully in chapter 3.

Italics Rate. Italics are another means of achieving emphasis or clarity. The practice is disfavored by many arbiters (for example, *The Chicago Manual of Style*) but is widely used.

Mean Number of Words in a Paragraph (Paragraph Mean).* We treat paragraphs as rhetorical structures that are signaled graphically by indentation or by other uses of spacing, although we recognize that this graphic signal is accompanied by linguistic signals in more skilled writers. As noted earlier, the paragraph mean is one of a cluster of interrelated stylistic devices which suggest how much of a burden the writer imposes upon the reader.

Standard Deviation of the Paragraph Mean (Paragraph S.D.). As with sentence and T-unit length, the paragraph mean must be put into the perspective of its variability. More skilled writers tend to have more variable paragraph means, since their prose is more flexible in finding the best option for expressing a particular idea. Thus, generally speaking, the larger the paragraph S.D., the more flexible and sophisticated the writer.

Category 5. Style

Percent of Passive-Voice Independent Clauses (Pct Passive). Passive-voice construction is frequently denigrated by belletristic stylists but is widely used in scientific, technical, and business writing. While it is frequently useful and legitimate in such settings, it can easily be overused, creating needlessly wordy sentences. In any case, it almost always implies less "personality" in the prose, whether it is the writer's self that is effaced or someone else's. We calculate the percent by dividing the number of passive-voice independent clauses by the total number of independent clauses.

Percent of Anticipatory-Construction Independent Clauses (Pct Anticipatory). Anticipatory constructions are those that begin with "It is," "There is," "There are," and so on. Like passive voice, they are shunned by belletristic writers and frequently employed by writers in business and technical writing.

Percent of "Framed" Independent Clauses (Pct Framed). In our usage, clauses are "framed" by introductory expressions such as "Figure 7 shows that . . ." or "I feel that . . ." Like passive-voice and anticipatory constructions, they are usually deemed wordy or inelegant by belletristic writers and are therefore shunned unless absolutely necessary.

Percent of "Weak" Independent Clauses (Pct Weak).* "Weak" is our catch-all term for independent clauses with passive-voice, anticipatory, or framed constructions.

Number of Personal Pronouns as a Percent of All Pronouns (Pct Personal). This measure was promoted by Rudolf Flesch (1951) as a measure of personality in a text and hence as an indicator of potential reader involvement. Although many scientific journals now urge or tolerate active voice (and with it the use of personal pronouns), the absence of personal pronouns is still typical of scientific and technical writing—or of any other writing in which self-effacement is prized.

Style Error Rate. Errors of style include all instances of weak clauses, as well as multiple embedding of clauses, "stacked" nouns (strings of nouns used as adjectives), grammatical expletives, nominalization, and weak repetition. The complete list of these errors that we looked for is shown in Appendix A.3. The measure is expressed as the rate of such errors per one hundred T-units.

Category 6. Usage

Usage Error Rate. * Usage errors, as we define them, consist of stylistic gaffes that do not much alter the clarity of ideas but that would be avoided by writers in the belletristic tradition. For a complete list of matters which we include in this category, see Appendix A.4. The measure is calculated as the rate of such errors per one hundred T-units.

Percent of Mispunctuated Structures (Pct Mispunctuations). Mispunctuated structures are those in which an inappropriate mark is used. This measure does not include *un*punctuated structures (unless a clause or phrase that should be nonrestrictive is not set off with a mark). The percent is calculated by dividing the number of mispunctuations by the total number of grammatical junctures calling for punctuation.

In addition to this analysis of the static stylistic aspects of each draft, the variables of revision operating to create each draft were documented in detail. Whenever a writer made a change in the text, we categorized it according to all seven variables, recording the change's impetus, item (including "old" item and "new," as appropriate), process, norm, affective impact, orientation, and goal. In addition, we recorded the effect of the change on the size of the text—whether the change increased it, decreased it, or left it the same size. Finally, we noted the "range" or number of structures involved in each change, and we added comments to explain clearly what the change was and what was of particular significance about it. If there was any question about the classification of a variable, a question mark was added to the code; all such items were later used to develop follow-up questions for the writers. Their responses were used to resolve questions about the coding of the variables for a particular revision.

The resulting computer files documenting the impetus, items (old and new), norm, affect, orientation, and goal operative in the production of each draft were thus conveniently stored for statistical analysis (rates and percentages) by another computer program designed by James Hoekstra of the Iowa State University Computation Center. The statistics generated included percentages and rates. For example, the numbers of idea, cohesion, style, usage, and high-affect changes in a proposal or draft were expressed first as a percent of the total number of changes; they were next expressed as rates per one hundred T-units for each proposal or draft. In chapter 4, we distinguish between our two writers (Baker and Franklin) mainly in terms of percents; we distinguish between drafts of a proposal mainly in terms of rates per one hundred T-units (based on the number of T-units in the text before the revisions for a particular draft were made).

To extend our analysis even further, the computer files of the text of each proposal's drafts were combined interlinearly into a single new file. Once the texts of each draft were brought together into one file, they could be sorted by computer so that each subsequent version of each structure would appear next to the original, in the following manner:

p 511 ,ad 1020.   After a long day in the forest
p 511 ,ad 2020.   After a 2r_hard_ day in the 2r_woods_

   631 ,ad 2020.5 2i_with little to show for their efforts_

```
010 . 5 1021.    the bears were tired and hungry
010 . 5 2021.    the bears were tired and hungry

s 611 ,ad 1022.    When they entered their home
s 611 ,ad 2022.    When they 2r_went inside_ their home

411 ,at  1023.    consequently
411 ,at  2023.    2r_therefore_
010 . 4  1024.    they were mad too
010 . 8  2024.    they 2i_soon_ 2r_became angry as well_
```

The resulting printout of the file allowed convenient, structure-by-structure comparison of revisions through traditional methods of explication and interpretation.

3

The Writing Environment of a
Management-Consulting Firm

To understand fully the composing and revising processes of the two writers analyzed in chapter 4, we first need to look at the institutional and generic norms of the company for which the management consultants worked. Consequently, this chapter describes several important aspects of that environment, including the ethos of the company (which we will hereafter call "the Firm"), the importance of writing in the organization, its proposal writing process, its audience, and some of the common strengths and weaknesses of its writers—in short, a variety of constraints, conditions, attitudes, behaviors, and technologies that influence the conception and execution of the Firm's documents. The analysis will serve as background for the subsequent examination of two of the Firm's individual writers in chapter 4, which will include further discussion of the norms the writers attempt to adhere to in composing their proposals.

The Firm

The Firm is an international management-consulting company whose clients include business and industrial concerns, colleges and universities, hospitals, professional societies, and federal, state, and foreign government agencies. Because the company works in manufacturing, logistics, strategy, human resources, and health care, the professional staff has a wide variety of academic backgrounds. Most have at least one postgraduate degree, and approximately ten percent have doctorates. From lowest to highest, their job titles are associate, manager, principal, and partner (which includes the titles vice-president and senior vice-president). All of the Firm's partners and principals are male. According to the *Journal of Management Consulting*, in 1981, the average salary for associates in management-consulting companies was about $40,000; that for senior partners ranged as high as $250,000.

The Firm has consulted for more than half of the Fortune 500 companies and, in the last five years, has completed more than five thousand assignments, most of which required a written proposal to secure the job. Thus, proposal writing is an extremely important activity at the Firm, and much of the organization's business depends upon the quality of proposals it writes and on the efficiency and proficiency of its proposal-writing process.

The Firm's Proposal-Writing Process

Before we can describe this process, it is important to distinguish between proposal writing in two different situations. First, if the client is a government agency, the writer's approach is highly formalized, primarily because state and federal departments generally follow a prescribed process for soliciting bids, communicating with the bidders, and evaluating their proposals. These agencies will often disseminate a detailed request for proposals (RFP) that provides bidders with the background, objectives, and scope of the problem and that details the procedures for submission and evaluation. In this situation, therefore, the methods and qualifications sections are usually more important than the background and objectives sections, because the agencies are most interested in the bidder's ability to solve the problem and manage the study. The proposals tend to be relatively more informative than persuasive, concentrating less on bonding with the readers (who are usually unknown anyway) and more on displaying the necessary technical expertise.

In the second situation, involving proposals written for the commercial sector, the writers are rarely presented with a substantive RFP; most often there is no RFP at all. Thus, the problem and its background must be uncovered through meetings with the client personnel, some of whom will have conflicting ideas about the nature of the problem because of their various job responsibilities, positions in the client company, fears or desires about their own jobs and the reputation of their departments, and so forth. Proposals responding to this situation, therefore, must present a highly informative and persuasive background section that places the problem in perspective and speaks to the needs and desires of the readers. Sometimes, however, the primary readers (those making the decision) and the methods by which they make the decision are unknown. Thus, the commercial-sector proposal generally presents the writer with more difficult rhetorical choices. The proposals analyzed later in this monograph were all written for the commercial sector, and it is the process of producing that kind of proposal that is described below.

The process begins when the Firm receives an inquiry from a client. At that point, a centralized department decides whether or not the Firm should respond to the bid. If the decision is to proceed, a team of people from different disciplines is assigned so that the Firm can best define the client's problem. The team includes a proposal manager, whose job it is to manage the proposal writing process; this person may or may not be the project officer who will manage the study if the proposal is successful. Criteria for selecting the team include the members' technical knowledge (area of expertise) and their availability to work on the proposal and to play key roles should the Firm acquire the assignment.

The whole purpose of the work thus far is to to make sure the job is appropriate and desirable for the Firm and to assign the best available personnel. Between the assignment of the team and the preparation of the proposal, members of the Firm meet with the client for several reasons: to make certain that the Firm has a full understanding of the scope of the job, the issues, and the objectives of the assignment; to discuss whether or not the perceived solutions may be the correct ones; to determine the role of the consultants and the extent to which the client's people will be involved in the study; and to establish rapport. At this time, members of the team analyze the audience as well as the task, gathering intelligence about the client's operational style—for example, whether or not the client works through committees, who the Firm will be accountable to (an individual or committee), who the members of the committee will be, what role that committee will play during the study, and so forth. In addition, the team members discover what data are available and what additional data will have to be gathered and prepared.

After the first meeting with the client, the proposal manager composes a strategy memo which describes the key players in the client company and identifies whether they are the decision makers or decision influencers. In addition, the memo indicates features that may need to be emphasized in the proposal, the possible themes that the proposal can be developed around (themes that respond to certain "hot buttons" detected during the interviews with the client), and the strategy that potential competitors for the job might adopt. Thus, one purpose of the strategy memo is to identify the obstacles to the Firm's getting the job and to sketch out a means of avoiding these obstacles.

Once the team members receive the strategy memo, they hold a strategy meeting. The meeting may involve only the members of the proposal team, or it may involve other members of the Firm who can provide constructive comments about the strategy for obtaining the job. After the first strategy meeting, there may be additional meetings with the client, as well as additional strategy sessions to deal with newly raised issues, to obtain additional information, to clarify points, and to determine how the Firm can best acquire the contract.

At this point, a draft of the proposal is generated, usually by one writer (either the project officer or someone selected by him), although sometimes a second writer contributes part or all of one of the main sections. This does not necessarily mean that there are no subsequent strategy meetings or further contacts with the client; it means that the Firm has at this point identified what it needs to present the proposal and to verify (perhaps through telephone conversation or on-site visits) that it has the necessary data and that the background information is correct.

After the proposal is written and presented, a debriefing session takes place, the purpose of which is to assess how well the proposal and the presentation were received and to decide how to maintain contact while the Firm is waiting for a response.

It is important to note that the process described above is a general, and sometimes idealized, version of what actually happens in the Firm. Sometimes there simply is not enough time to engage in all of the steps. Sometimes only one person writes the proposal, and no strategy sessions are held or strategy memos written. Sometimes the client decides to have an additional study done, a continuation study, and no proposal as such even needs to be written. That is, every situation is in some ways unique, and every proposal and the process used to gather data for it and write it must respond to that uniqueness.

The Firm's Proposals

The scope and size of the Firm's proposals are as various as the situations they respond to. Some are three-volume, several-hundred-page, bound documents for $30 million, three-year studies for governmental agencies. These proposals may take as long as two months to research and write. They may involve ten subcontractors. The entire proposal writing team may number fifteen people. Other proposals, on the other hand, may be seven-page, single-spaced letters for $250,000 studies to Fortune 500 companies. Others might be $25,000 studies for local businesses. Some proposals are extraordinarily well written and ultimately successful; others are poorly written but still end up getting the job.

Despite the differences in size and scope, the Firm's proposals typically are arranged into three main sections, each of which may consist of one or more of the following parts:

Problem
 Introduction
 Background
 Objectives
 Scope
 Study Strategy
Method
 Approach
 Deliverables
Implementation
 Staffing and Qualifications
 Timing
 Cost
 Conclusion

The first main section—which we call the "problem" section—invariably begins with an introduction that refers to previous discussions about the project and expresses the Firm's interest in it. A "background" part discusses the client's problem and need for a solution. An "objectives and scope" part (which may or may not be set off with its own heading) lists the main and secondary study objectives and discusses the limits of the study. A "study strategy" part provides a rationale explaining why the proposed approach was selected and why it is the best one.

The second main section, which we call the "method" section, consists primarily of a part called the "approach," which details the worksteps and indicates, if necessary, how the study will be phased. A part on "deliverables" identifies the outputs to be delivered to the client at the end of the project; these could include a final report, procedure manuals, maps, detailed exhibits, and so on.

In the third main section, which we call the "implementation" section, a part called "staffing" or "qualifications" details the Firm's relevant experience with similar projects and the particular experience of the proposed team members; sometimes an extended description of personnel is added in an appendix devoted to qualifications. Next, a "timing and costs" part identifies the study's beginning and ending dates and details the project's cost and the method of payment; though short, this part is important for legal reasons. Finally, the implementation section concludes the proposal with another expression of interest in the project and confidence in the Firm's ability to carry out the task.

As noted above, not all of these sections are used in every proposal, nor are they always labeled as such. One $400,000 proposal to one of the country's largest corporations, for example, had no "objectives" section, primarily because the study's issues were so many and the study itself so complex that the objectives could be developed only after the project was well underway. Moreover, in the same proposal, the "approach" section was not named as such: because one of the proposal's themes emphasized the ability of the Firm to work intimately with the client's personnel, the section was titled "How We Can Work Together."

The proposal might be bound and accompanied by a cover letter or it might be in letter form itself. If a letter, it is usually designed in narrative format (that is, with standard paragraphing). If bound, it might be in narrative or in presentation format, in which the guts are composed of the hard copy of slides given at an oral presentation. Presentation format reflects the values that the business culture places on brevity and conciseness and its preferences for the visual rather than for the "written." The format looks like this:

—Presentation format is sometimes called:

• Bullet Point

• Dot-Dash

• Outline

—It is characterized by clean lines and white space to:

• Highlight important information

• Make that information accessible to the busy executive

Because each project manager or officer may prefer one format over another, some of the Firm's proposal writers almost always write their proposals in the same format. Other writers, however, decide on a format based primarily on their perceptions of their readers. Because each of the Firm's offices has developed its own traditions and practices, some offices use one kind of format more often than others do.

The Importance of Audience

Implicit in the description of the Firm's proposal-writing process is the importance placed on the consultants' knowledge of their readers. Consulting is a highly personal business, and clients buy consulting services based on two major criteria: the technical expertise of the Firm and the personal relationship between consultant and client. That is, if clients are going to spend several hundred thousand dollars for consulting services, they must be sure that the working relationships are sound. Often, therefore, the consultant wins a job not merely because of technical expertise (since most of the top agencies are experts in their fields) but because the client believes, through personal contact as well as through the image and voice projected in the proposal, that the consultant can work effectively with the client. Indeed, some of the senior-level consultants—those who do the majority of the proposal writing—believe that clients rarely make a rational decision when contracting for consulting services. Thus, just as important as the "hard issues" of technical expertise and method of approach are the soft issues dealing with human motivation and feeling.

One proposal writer's understanding of those soft issues is suggested by the following interview transcript—one which shows, incidentally, how knowledge of audience (in this case, a Fortune 500 company) can determine how a proposal is presented:

> Did I ever tell you about the icebergs—about the XYZ proposal? A young fellow who is an internal consultant for them invited us in in a competitive situation to talk about inventory with them. We had a long meeting with him and then a long second meeting, and then we had to write a proposal to go with him to his boss.
>
> I hate that kind of situation. We have never met his boss; all we know is his boss is a hard-charging, young, very creative guy who, as all the other top people at XYZ, shot up in the organization. And I said, "Does he like presentations, or does he like written documents?" The internal consultant said, "He gets annoyed at too many words and things; he likes creative presentations."
>
> We put together a presentation with about twenty-five pages, a little flip chart thing which I would put on the boss's desk, so I was totally in control. It was mostly cartoons and all kinds of wild things, a lot of meaning and very few words. At the end, there was a cartoon, and it showed a boat and the captain of the boat sort of leaning over the front, and it said "XYZ Management" on the captain. (Sounds really dumb!) And out there are a bunch of icebergs and the tops of the icebergs say things like "reduce inventory" or "cut inventory costs," and on the bottom, "destroy customer confidence," and on the very top of the cartoon I wrote, "Our objective is to steer you through these icebergs, avoid some of them, go right through some because they are so small that they don't make any difference, and show you where to set dynamite charges to get rid of the really bad ones."
>
> Now the internal consultant asked me for a copy of this in advance, so I sent him a letter, giving him the philosophy of what we were trying to do and so forth, and word by word I explained that whole last cartoon.

At the meeting, I flipped through the charts and when I flipped to the last one, I said, "It's sort of like icebergs," and then didn't say anything, and suddenly the internal consultant said, "Yes, as a matter of fact . . ." and he just came right through and he independently quoted right from our little personal letter to him, which really was the proposal. Now, he looked smart. His boss liked it, and we got the job. Now, if he wouldn't have said anything, I would have kept talking. But we made him part of the creative team without soliciting it. He could be part of our team, which he wanted to be, he could be smart in front of his boss, and be selling his boss. Anyhow, that was the iceberg story.

To analyze their audience, the consultants attempt to answer many questions during the strategy sessions and in the strategy memos. Concerning the client's problem, they try to determine what the nature of the problem is, how important and urgent the problem is, whether the issues involved are symptoms of the problem or the problem itself, and whether the clients know which are the symptoms and which the problem. Concerning the competition, they try to determine who the competition is, whether the competition has done previous work for the client, and if so, what opinion the client had of that work. In light of that analysis, they decide on those unique selling points that will differentiate them from the competition, and then determine how those selling points can be expressed as themes or key ideas—short, simple words and phrases that will trigger a reader's affective as well as cognitive response. Concerning the client personnel and their attitudes, the consultants try to identify the prospective client players—whether they are major decision makers or influencers, what their expectations and hidden agendas might be, and what risks they and their company face if the problem is not solved. In addition, the consultants try to determine how the players feel about consultants, particularly about the Firm and the individuals who might be on its consulting team. If possible, the consultants also identify criteria to be used in evaluating the proposal and the personnel who will evaluate it, including people they might not have had the opportunity to meet.

All this information is necessary if the proposal is to have a good chance of winning the job. That is, the proposal must focus on the client's goals and demonstrate the consultant's knowledge of the client's situation, so that the proposal "feeds back" the needs, desires, and wishes of the client. Furthermore, the proposal must be congruent with the message and image of the firm presented to the client during previous face-to-face meetings.

Because of the intense personal nature of the proposal-writing process, the importance of this congruence cannot be overemphasized. If the proper relationship between consultant and client has been established during the earlier stages of the process, the job can be substantially sold even before the proposal is delivered. But if a proposal does not convey the same tone and message, the same "feeling" communicated to the client during the face-to-face conversations, then it stands a good chance of losing rather than winning the job. In fact, those initial contacts are so important that some of the Firm's senior people believe the proposal does not itself sell the job, but that, by the time it is written, it can only clinch or lose the job. This is perhaps an odd notion in academic circles, where the proposal or grant application may be the first and last step in securing funds.

Because some jobs are sold "upfront," the Firm sometimes writes a subgenre of proposals called "confirming letters," which function as little more than legally binding contracts documenting the previously agreed-upon objectives, scope, approach, and timing and costs of the study. Nevertheless, many of the Firm's proposals must be very persuasive documents, and especially in highly competitive situations, these proposals are instrumental in securing contracts.

Writing Problems at the Firm

Twenty years ago, according to one senior vice-president, the consulting staff probably had to produce, "per capita," considerably more writing than they do today. Then, nearly all the proposals and reports were written in narrative format, and a typical report may have run two hundred and fifty pages. Because these long documents required so much writing, the Firm's employees received more practice in writing—and also more instruction in writing, since informal teacher-student relationships tended to evolve during the massive document production efforts. Even though today's more visual formats require less writing, the consultants spend about 25 percent of their time composing proposals, strategy memos, final reports, and other documents. But if "writing" also includes the time studying clients' problems and thus researching for their proposals and reports, then the figure is probably closer to 75 percent. Thus, writing proficiency is an extremely important skill in the Firm, and the writers know it. In a survey of thirty of the Firm's employees, 93 percent strongly agreed (none strongly disagreed) that skill in written communication was important to their professional development and advancement.

Considering the importance placed on writing, it is not surprising that many of the consultants believe that they write well and with relatively little pain and effort. Thirty-three percent strongly agreed that they are good writers, 43 percent that they enjoy the writing they do at work, and 23 percent that writing is a relatively efficient process for them. Fewer than 6 percent strongly disagreed in any of these categories. Twenty-six percent rarely considered writing a chore, and only 3 percent often did. None indicated that they feel uneasy about how their reader will respond to their writing.

Few of the writers display significant problems with grammar and mechanics. Occasionally, a lack of agreement between subject and verb or between pronoun and antecedent occurs; sometimes there is an awkward shift in voice, a semicolon used where a colon is necessary, or a lack of appropriate parallelism (especially in lists). One of the most common "errors," though few of the consultants would consider it as such and perhaps no one but a prescriptive grammarian should worry about it, is a dangling introductory element followed by a main clause in passive voice. For example: "To understand Acme's marketing potential, a thorough analysis of the potential end-users will be conducted." On the whole, few of their problems exist at the sentence level.

Generally speaking, they have no problems in getting started to write either. They *have* to get started quickly and to write under the intense pressure of strict deadlines. Those who cannot are in the wrong business, simply unsuited to a profession whose members fill file drawers, three feet wide, with their proposals and reports; who write, when business is booming, more than twenty proposals a year; and who sometimes have to write them in one to three days. We have seen excellent, individually written, twenty-five-page reports composed in a week; well-written fifteen-page proposals composed in a day. Although 23 percent of the writers surveyed did say they often have problems in getting started to write, most of them claimed one reason: lack of technical command of their subject matter. Given the rapidity with which they must write, it is understandable that most are unanxious about writing or having to write. Fifty-six percent marked "rarely" and none marked "often" in response to the statement: "Writing makes me uneasy."

Interestingly, the writers do not know what to do about the writing problems they do have—at least those they are aware of. Only three percent, for example, strongly agreed that they know how to solve their problems in writing. This is an interesting statistic, considering that the consultants make their living as problem solvers. Almost daily they analyze clients' logistic and manufacturing processes, marketing strategies, and managerial behaviors, and yet they rarely use that expertise to improve their own writing processes and behaviors or the Firm's document production process. Although 30 percent strongly agreed that they consciously try to improve their writing skills, only 3 percent strongly agreed with the statement: "I think about solving my writing problems in much the same way I might help a client solve problems."

Our discussion of writing problems at the Firm will focus on two areas: those problems caused by the writers themselves and those caused by the Firm's process of producing documents. The first area focuses primarily on audience-related problems, those stemming from insufficient or inappropriate audience analysis and adaptation. The second area focuses on systemic problems, those stemming from errors or inefficiencies within the Firm's system of document production. The discussion is intended to be indicative rather than exhaustive, serving to preview and anticipate some of the findings and conclusions presented in the following chapters.

Audience-Related Problems

We know, of course, that most successful writers analyze their audience and adapt their documents accordingly and that one of the most important failings of unsuccessful writers is the lack of appropriate adaptation to audience. Indeed, except for basic errors in grammar and mechanics, nearly every problem in a document could be seen as audience-related, including inappropriate style and tone, ineffective structure and organization, insufficient or extraneous information, incorrect level of technicality, and so forth. Not surprisingly, all of these often-discussed audience-related problems can be found in the Firm's documents. We wish to examine two less-discussed kinds of unadapted writing: boilerplating and writer-based prose.

Boilerplating. One of the most significant audience-related problems at the Firm involves "boilerplating," which occurs when writers lift passages from one document (either their own or somebody else's) and insert them into the document they are composing. The lifted material, which can range from a distinctive phrase to a very large stretch of discourse, most often occurs in qualifications, methods, and budget sections.

Although boilerplate can be useful in assuring writers a legally accurate statement of company policy and in saving writers time and effort by providing template descriptions of common processes and rationales, it can be problematic for two reasons. First, when passages appropriate for one rhetorical situation are inserted into a document responding to another, boilerplate can result in a collision of styles and tones. Its use thus becomes a big problem for those less-skilled writers who cannot detect subtle stylistic and tonal differences. Second, boilerplating is a problem because, when it is done habitually, it tends to remove the writer from the rhetorical situation. That is, when writers boilerplate, they tend to forget about the needs of their intended audience, momentarily failing to consider the unique needs of the situation and the unique selling points they are trying to communicate. Thus, boilerplating can become an escape from thinking and an excuse for not thinking. It becomes a crutch, offering apparently simple solutions to rhetorical problems that are ultimately much more complex.

The problems with boilerplating are evident in a recently written document proposing to design a compensation program for a client—not just any compensation program, but one specifically tailored to the unique needs of the client's organization. Unfortunately, one section was obviously boilerplated— the very section that tried to convince the reader that the Firm did not have canned approaches for solving the problem. As a result, the Firm's credibility might have been severely undermined because the proposal railed against canned programs in a passage that was obviously canned. We cannot be sure, of course, if the readers detected this duplicity, or if they did, whether that was the reason for the job's being lost.

The better of the Firm's writers are not only able to adapt boilerplate well but to determine when boilerplate of any kind will be inappropriate. These writers have a much more sophisticated understanding of the demands of rhetoric: they know that each proposal must respond to a unique situation. The following anecdote, from one of the Firm's best writers, is instructive:

> I wrote a proposal last week that I thought was going to be exactly like another proposal I wrote for another company. It is in the same industry, the same products, the same size specifications, almost the exact same geographic area. I pulled out that other proposal in order to boilerplate from it. I thought this would be a cake walk. But by the time I was done, the only thing the other proposal did was to supply some neat ideas for me.
>
> They were just totally different because the other proposal was for a company that I had done ten or twelve studies for before. It was for the president that I knew very well, whose son was also a client of mine, and there was this relationship, a little better than a client relationship, and his company was fantastically successful. But this one was for a company where I had never met anybody; the company was in trouble; there was no warm feeling; there was no ten years of experience; there were no previous assignments.
>
> The previous proposal was sort of a "Hey, Stan, this sort of confirms what we will do together, and we will do our best and if we blow it we will change in midstream, and it has been great seeing you and the wife kind of thing." But this current one is, "(1) you don't know me, (2) I have to establish my credentials and my firm's credentials, (3) we are sorry we took so long to respond, because we lost your letter (which is really #4); of all the firms you talked to, however, we are the only ones with the exact right qualifications—here they are," and now, suddenly, we have a totally different proposal.

Writer-Based Prose. Lack of audience adaptation is evident in some interesting passages of writer-based prose. These passages often appear in the methods sections, where the writers describe the tasks or worksteps to be performed during the proposed study. Here are four typical examples taken from four different worksteps in the final draft of one proposal:

> This requires that our understanding of all Acme operations must be comprehensive.

A good understanding of its operation and past results is necessary to do this effectively.

In developing the salaried plan concept at Acme, it will be important to understand the XXX salary bonus plan.

To properly evaluate the potential impact of various incentive concepts on Acme operations, it will be necessary to have an organized, comprehensive summary of improvement opportunities.

Characteristic of these passages is their self-reflexiveness. That is, the author is not so much transacting with a reader as he is talking to himself, as if he were saying: "It will be necessary for *me* to have an organized, comprehensive summary if *I* am to evaluate the incentive concepts properly." These final-draft passages are traces of the writer's "conversations" with himself when in the earlier drafts he was essentially reminding himself of what *he* should be sure to do in the study, rather than what he would do for the client. In two instances, the passages contain a broad pronoun reference ("this"), which may be a sign of egocentric discourse, since such references do not appear elsewhere in the proposal—only in the "methods" section.

The writer-based passages may tend to occur in "methods" because the aim of that section is primarily informative and does not require, at least from the writer's point of view, that it create and sustain an argument: the line of thought is more logical than psychological. Moreover, "methods" is easily generated through outlining and listing as the writer attempts initially to answer his own question "What will I do?" rather than focusing, as he eventually should, on the reader's question "What will you do for me?" Consequently (as we will see later), writers may tend to make a lower percentage of reader-based ("high-affect" revisions) in the methods section than in a persuasive section such as the background. In chapter 4, we will be able to examine similar passages and observe from draft to draft their gradual transformation to reader-based prose.

Systemic Problems

Just as it is difficult to evaluate transactional discourse apart from its rhetorical situation, it is difficult if not unrealistic to analyze an organization's written products without understanding the organization producing that writing. For some writing problems exist in the organization precisely because it is an organization, a document production system, whose methods, values, and exigencies affect the quality and quantity of writing produced. These systemic problems are caused by the physical constraints of the environment, by the cultural constraints of the company's traditions, beliefs, and values, and by the administrative and managerial constraints stemming from the way the Firm goes about its business.

Physical Constraints of the Environment. Despite the amount of collaborative writing done in the business world, the fact remains that writing is primarily a solitary activity. Teams of writers can plan their strategies, provisionally decide upon the structure and design of the document, and review their colleagues' drafts. But the drafting itself—and the necessary incubation before and during the drafting—usually takes place, and for many writers must take place, in isolation. Thus, the writer's environment, the architectural space in which writing is done, can be very important.

The partners and principals of the Firm have rather large and spacious offices that can be closed off from the noisy distractions of hallway conversations, printers, and photocopying machines. At some of the regional offices, however, the associates and managers have their desks in "open space" environments consisting of row after row of cubicles similar to library carrels. Imagine, then, the dilemma facing an associate at one of the regional offices. He or she sits in a cubicle surrounded by other cubicles, and there must write. As he or she tries to complete a section of a report and to meet a tight deadline, colleagues' phones are ringing, the associate in the next cubicle is having a very interesting phone conversation, one secretary is typing, the printer is printing, the photocopy machine has just gone down and an operator is cursing it, and two partners standing close by are having a casual conversation about a possible job to which the associate hopes to be assigned.

It is true, of course, that many writers do write, and write well, in "open space" environments, the large newsroom being a good example where writers must perform despite numerous distractions. But it is also true that several of the Firm's writers find it exceedingly difficult to compose in such environments, often having to write their documents after hours, sometimes at home.

Cultural Constraints. The physical constraints of the environment are problems in themselves, of course, but they are also a symptom of a larger problem: the Firm's failure to regard the professional staff as writers. It is true that the Firm does recognize the importance of writing *skills.* It offers a tutorial-based program in written communication as well as workshops in proposal writing, and it includes a section on writing competence in the employees' annual performance review. But in some important ways, the organization does not have a sense of itself as being composed of individuals who write a good deal for their living and for the Firm's livelihood.

Most professional writers, for example, have no bias against using typewriters, which are as much a part of the mythos of the writer's environment as scotch and despair. But the Firm's consultants tend to believe that typewriters are for secretaries and computer keyboards are for word-processing operators. Therefore, one rarely sees typewriters or computer terminals in the consultants' offices. Many of the consultants do have personal computers at home, but few use computers at work—and even then, they use them for number crunching, not for word processing. Thus, although one would expect many of the professional staff to be composing their documents at terminals or desk computers, such is not the case.

This cultural bias against typing determines in several ways how documents are produced at the Firm. First, those who do not dictate their first drafts must write them out by hand, submit the drafts for typing, receive the typescript, proofread and revise by hand, wait again for the new output, perhaps revise again, and so forth. Thus, turnaround time is increased because the word-processing operator must type into a file what the writer has already written and because the writer must proofread each draft of the typist's output. Second, because the writer must give over his writing to the word-processing operator, he or she no longer maintains control over format and usage, but places himself at the mercy of the organization's style guide. Third, the lack of access to CRTs makes it more difficult to manage collaborative writing efforts. If the proposal writing team composed its documents on integrated hardware, it could send the drafts electronically to the proposal manager, who could easily assemble and revise them.

Another cultural bias is partly responsible for the fact that the

Firm does not have in-house editors or professional writers. Such employees could offer counsel on how important documents could be designed and organized and how possible themes or selling points could be incorporated. They could also play a principal role in revising and polishing the drafts. The Firm does have what is called an "editor," but that person's job is primarily to proofread. There are no in-house professional writers for two reasons. First, many of the consultants do not see the advantage of using them (though clearly, in a great many cases, the writers could make substantial contributions). Second, some of the consultants do not believe that an in-house writer could stand up to the inevitable abuse. "She," some have said, perhaps indicating the perceived lowliness of the position by the sex they think the writer would be, "would have to be a *very* strong personality to deal with the kind of people at the Firm." The bias against an in-house writer is probably changing as the consultants begin to realize the contributions he or she could make as well as the contributions "technical writers" *are* making at other companies.

Administrative and Managerial Constraints. To present a detailed description of all the Firm's systemic problems related to its document production process would require a very long chapter indeed, for even the most apparently trivial problems in writing can stem from inefficiencies or errors in the document production system. We can consider, for example, two of what at first appear to be minor problems in some of the Firm's documents: absence of the final comma separating items in a series; and lack of descriptive tabs indicating major sections in bound proposals and reports.

The first problem arises in the Firm's central word-processing unit, where the operators are instructed never to use a comma before the "and" coordinating the last element in a series. Thus, even if a writer's first draft used commas to separate each element in a series of three (for example, "Tom, Dick, and Harry"), the comma before "and" would be deleted by the word-processing unit. There are occasions, of course, when eliminating the final comma could result in ambiguity, as in the following example:

Background, Objectives, Methods and Timing and Costs are major sections in the Firm's proposals.

Without prior knowledge, it is difficult if not impossible here to know whether the last two major sections are "methods" and "timing and costs" or "methods and timing" and "costs." Yet some of the Firm's writers, even when they are aware of such an ambiguity, will not insert the final comma because they know that their typescript will come back with the comma deleted. They would rather give in to the system than fight it, so they rarely make the effort to keep the commas in.

The second problem has its roots in the graphics department. For long, bound proposals and reports—those requiring tabs between the major sections—the graphics department is responsible for making the tabs. Its preprinted labels, however, do not consist of functional, reader-oriented words and phrases such as "background," "objectives," or "timing and costs"; instead, they consist of nonfunctional headings such as "Section I," "Section II," and so on. Thus, unless a writer wishes his bound proposal to be tabbed otherwise, and to waste precious time having the graphics department create special labels, it will come back to him with the usual tabs.

This can be an important problem once we realize how the document might be used. Let us assume that the client has received five proposals, has eliminated all but two—the Firm's and a major competitor's, and is meeting to select a finalist. The chair of the meeting wishes the committee to evaluate both agencies' approaches to the study and therefore requests that the committee open each proposal to the "methods" section. Because the competitor's proposal has a tab labeled "methods," the committee members quickly turn to that section. To find that section in the Firm's proposal, however, the committee must turn over the cover, the inside cover page, and a two-page letter of transmittal before coming to the table of contents, which lists "Section III: Methods." Only then can the committee members locate the methods section. This difficulty might well have a negative effect on the committee, and since the committee is to hire a management-consulting agency (for several hundred thousand dollars) to solve a problem that their own company cannot solve, they want *problem solvers*. But the committee has just been presented with a problem—finding the methods section—which the rival consulting agency solved effortlessly while the Firm did not. If, as we stated before, the clients do not necessarily make rational decisions, their choice might be influenced by the vague labels on the tabs.

These problems illustrate two important points about writing in organizational settings. First, many small problems and some big ones that occur in a company's documents are caused not so much by the writer as by the system that produces his or her writing. Second, the system can condition writers, causing them not to trouble with bucking the system and in time, perhaps, not to think about being troubled. Thus, as we turn now to an examination of two writers and the multi-draft proposals they composed, it is important to keep in mind that the writers' work not only responds to the perceived needs of its readers; it also responds to and is powerfully conditioned by the norms and traditions of the writers' own organization.

4

The Composing / Revising Processes
of Two Management Consultants

TWO MEMBERS OF THE FIRM DESCRIBED IN CHAPTER 3 COULD provide us with complete records of four proposals that they had recently written. In this chapter, we will describe the social, professional, and personal characteristics of the two writers, along with their conceptions of their writing strategies and habits. Then we will analyze the eight proposals in terms of process (the seven variables described in chapter 1) and product (the quantifiable aspects of style described in chapter 2). For reasons of confidentiality, we will refer to the management consultants who participated in our study as Baker and Franklin; we will refer to Baker's proposals as Bak-A, Bak-B, Bak-C, and Bak-D, and to Franklin's as Fra-A, Fra-B, Fra-C, and Fra-D.

The Writers' Characteristics:

Since the institutional and generic norms influencing the two writers were treated fully in chapter 3, we will here focus on cultural and personal factors.

Cultural Norms
Baker is a 40-year-old, upper-middle-class, white male. He is well educated, holding a B.S. (industrial engineering) and an M.B.A., both from prestigious midwestern universities. He is also experienced, having been a management consultant for fourteen years.

For the last several years, he has been a vice-president of the Firm, subordinate in most matters only to the Firm's president and its chair of the board. So far as his formal training in composition is concerned, he took a freshman-level course while a senior in high school but had no writing course in college; thus, his competence in linguistic matters such as cohesion and usage is a product of general cultural experience rather than special instruction.

Franklin is a sixty-one-year old white male and is also a vice-president of the Firm. He holds Bachelor of Science degrees in aeronautical engineering and mechanical engineering from a Big Ten university. He has been with the Firm for sixteen years and previously worked for three large corporations for fifteen years. His area of expertise is manufacturing strategy, which includes the fields of facility planning and location (site selection). As a result of his work in these areas, he has adapted for the Firm computerized transportation cost models and developed two computerized data banks. He has also written several articles and a book related to his work at the Firm. His formal training in composition consisted of two semesters of freshman English in college.

Personal Norms

Baker's conception of the writing process reflects not only a culturally nurtured rhetorical strategy ("plan, generate, alter"), and not only the Firm's general procedure for securing contracts, but also an idiosyncratic, visually conceived understanding of the creative process that he acquired from his college minor in art. Baker said of one of his drawing teachers:

> The guy that headed the department was aggravating because he would ask you to do impossible things and every time you got overly confident, he would ask you to do something more impossible, and suddenly, at the end you realized that you could do all those impossible things. But his standard thing was: "I want you to sketch this—and you have two minutes, you have five minutes." It was never more than five minutes. Once, at the end of the semester it was fifteen minutes and we all went crazy. For instance, we would go to the top of a hill looking down on a village and a river, and you can't believe around the second or third or fifth time how well you can sketch in two minutes.

Baker recommends a similar practice in sketching the key issues later to be articulated in his proposals:

> Take one minute alone (because I don't think you can do it in a group) . . . take one minute alone and write down the major issues. Take one minute alone and write down the unique things we could do that some other company can't do in dealing with those issues. Take one minute alone and write down the key in one or two words, the key steps to make sure those issues fit into solving that problem. Maybe even take one minute to say, "Identify your client's 1-2-3 worst individual concerns, etc."

Because of this "sketch-pad" approach to writing, Baker's typical composing strategy is to generate at least a whole section of the proposal at a time, send that section off to the word-processing unit for a typescript, generate the next section, and so on. When the first typescript is returned, he revises it as a whole, and sends the corrected copy back for a fresh typescript. Usually, he revises in ink, with very few false starts or strike-overs for his emendations. For all but one of his proposals (Bak-D), his composing/revising strategy produced at least three typescripts, even though the actual time spent in composing the document was less than eight hours. It is important to bear in mind, however, that this is his general pattern; in nearly every proposal, his practice was altered somewhat by the demands of the rhetorical situation, as we will show in some detail later on.

Before writing his first draft, Franklin generally goes back over his notes from the preproposal meeting or meetings and then decides what sections the proposal will have—for example, whether it will have a section on deliverables or qualifications. Then he "feeds" the information from the preproposal meeting into the various proposal segments "to make sure that I'm being responsive, that I have a good strong background statement, that I spell out the objectives we agreed to."

Franklin remarks that he does not often move text around in his document, that the line of thought contained in the first draft is pretty much the organizational pattern in the final copy. "I know that I want to start here and I want to end up over there," he says.

He tries to think through the logic of the proposal ahead of time: "When I get that first draft back . . . I really don't anticipate any major changes." According to Franklin, his minor textual changes involve alterations for "clarity," "readability," "flow," "simplicity," and "tone": "If I want to be real authoritative and show a company who does not know us—really try to get across the point that we know what we're about and what we're doing, then my tone might be a little bit different. Maybe a little more technical and more authoritative. But basically readability and sentence structure and simplicity."

Just as Franklin's ideas about writing are more conventional than Baker's, his writing process is less complex, in the sense that he creates fewer drafts. Franklin composes the first draft on lined paper, in pencil. His second drafts consist of penciled emendations, sometimes over part of a passage that he has just written, but more usually over longer stretches of the text. This pencil draft with penciled revisions is then sent to the word-processing unit for a typescript copy, which is typically revised once and then sent out to the client.

Prose Style

Nearly every measure of style indicates that, relatively speaking, Baker's writing is more sophisticated and probably more readable than Franklin's (see Appendix C.1 and C.2). To put it another way, Baker's prose more nearly resembles that of professional writers of the sort that Francis Christensen described—the writers in *Atlantic Monthly* and similar magazines whose authors are highly skilled. In terms of academic writing, Baker's prose has many of the characteristics associated with humanities teachers and scholars (particularly those who write about literature), whereas Franklin employs the stylistic strategies common in scientific and technical fields. This difference is evident in measures of complexity, variability, variety, linguistic and graphic cohesion, and style and usage.

Complexity. Both writers have long T-units, compared to college freshmen, with Franklin's 21.9 average being a little over two words longer per T-unit than Baker's 19.7. More important than the length of the T-unit, however, is the degree to which the T-unit is segmented into more easily comprehended structures. In this respect, Baker's independent clauses are, on average, more than three words shorter than Franklin's (14.7 versus 17.9), so that, assuming an equality of other factors (for example, the familiarity or abstractness of vocabulary, or the internal organization of clauses), we would expect Baker's prose to be easier to read than Franklin's. Another common measure of complexity makes this conclusion even more likely: in every 100 T-units, Baker has only 30 bound clauses (subordinate or relative clauses not set off by punctuation), whereas Franklin has 43 bound clauses per 100 T-units. Again, other factors being equal, we would expect Baker's kind of complexity to be easier for readers to process than Franklin's.

Variability. Although Franklin's T-units are longer than Baker's, Baker's are more variable in length and thus presumably more adapted to the flow of ideas (as we will note in discussing variety and cohesion).

Variety. It is difficult to compare the variety of syntactic elements in Baker's and Franklin's writings, since Baker's texts are so much larger than Franklin's—a disparity which tends to skew any comparison. That is, if one person speaks one thousand words and another one hundred, we would expect the one-thousand-word speaker to use a wider vocabulary, simply because the opportunity to do so is so much expanded by the greater number of words. This is true, however, only when the number of possible choices is very large. That is, when choosing one hundred or one thousand words to speak, a writer may draw from a linguistic reservoir of hundreds of thousands of words. But if we shift our attention from words to grammatical structures, then an opposite limitation comes into play, since the number of available grammatical structures is extremely small compared to the number of words (as noted in chapter 2, we distinguish only twenty kinds of structure and only thirty-two internal patterns for independent clauses). Under these circumstances, it becomes more likely that, in the first 100 T-units, the variety of structures will be greater than in the second 100 clauses. That is, in the first 100 structures, the ten most frequent structures might be used, along with five less frequently occurring ones. In the second 100 T-units, the number of T-units increases by 100, but the number of kinds of structures used can *at most* increase by five. The only answer to this problem is to compare finite and equal quantities— the first 100 T-units of Baker's texts with the first 100 T-units of Franklin's, for example. Again, however, the difference in the sizes of their texts intervenes, since the first 100 T-units of a proposal by Baker generally consists entirely of exposition and argumentation, whereas the first 100 T-units of Franklin's much shorter proposals contain not only these modes but also narrative patterns. So far as variety of kinds of structures and kinds of clausal patterns are concerned, therefore, it would be impossible to tell whether we were comparing writers or modes of writing. In any event, compared to Franklin, Baker uses (on the average) more kinds of structures and more patterns of clauses (22 vs. 17), as shown in Appendix C.1. While no definite conclusion about variety of structural kinds may be drawn, Baker's possibly greater variety may also reflect greater sophistication, greater adaptation of the form of the text to its content.

Another measure yields clearer distinctions: the variety of positions in which free modifiers occur. Both writers use about the same percent of initial-position free modifiers, but Franklin uses more middle-position FMs, while Baker uses more final-position FMs and also more free modifiers within other free modifiers. In this respect, too, Baker approaches a more literary configuration of stylistic elements and Franklin a more scientific or technical one.

Linguistic Cohesion. In using a wider variety of structures, Baker proves to be more ready to develop an idea by means of a final-position free modifier; in the same situation, Franklin is more likely to develop the idea in a new sentence, linking the first and second sentences with a transitional free modifier in initial position. For example, in the following passages, Baker employs a free modifier (-*ing* verb cluster, or present participial phrase) whose key word is "using," while Franklin relies on a new sentence whose key phrase is "we will use":

> We will develop an initial budget for marketing, using historical cost information and projections developed from discussions, salary ranges and estimated support costs. (Baker)

> In this task, we will examine each of those areas identified as having the greatest potential impact on the effectiveness of manufacturing operations. To study these areas, we will use a variety of techniques such as:
>   −observations
>   −interviews
>   −analysis of reports, procedures, practices
>   −data collection and analysis. (Franklin)

Similarly, while both use echoing or parallel cohesive free modifiers, such as a sentence-opening phrase ("Second, we will") echoing
a similar construction that opened a previous sentence ("First, we
will"), Baker is much more likely to signal the similarity between
ideas in different sentences by casting the sentences into echoing
developmental free modifiers, as in this sequence from Bak-A (in
which the structures that echo are in italics):

> *Using the market research data accumulated from the interviews* . . . ,
> we will develop a white paper. . . .

> *Using the perspective of the interviews* . . . , we will refine the long-
> range plan. . . .

> *Using the objective previously developed and presented to Directors*, re-
> view the conceptual alternatives. . . .

> *Working closely with selected management representatives*, we will de-
> velop much of the supporting detail. . . .

> *Using the responsibility matrix*, a plan can be developed to assure that all
> functions are assigned and none are duplicated.

> *Using comparisons from other firms*, we will establish reasonable ranges
> of compensation for each marketing position.

Even though Baker uses such echoing developmental free modifiers
and clauses more frequently than Franklin does, he still does not
exploit all such opportunities. For example, in the sequence just illustrated, he twice lapses from the echoing "we will" clausal frame—
once into a "minor" or incomplete clause ("review the conceptual
alternatives," rather than "we will review the conceptual alternatives"), and once into passive voice ("a plan can be developed,"
rather than "we will develop a plan").

In regard to another technique of linguistic cohesion, both writers
use about the same number of cohesive ties (whether bound or free)
and about the same proportion of cohesive free modifiers. Baker,
however, is much more consistent in this respect, varying very little
from text to text, whereas Franklin's identical percentage masks a

much greater variability, some proposals having relatively few cohesive ties (Fra-A, Fra-D) and one (Fra-B) having a very high number.

Another cohesive device—pronouns—is used more frequently by Franklin (172 per 100 T-units) than by Baker (132 per 100 T-units). Again, this emphasis on pronouns reflects Franklin's tendency to develop an idea in a separate sentence or clause (using a pronoun to refer back to the first sentence, as in the example above), instead of using a verbal or nominal free modifier that would need no pronoun.

Franklin makes more frequent use of another signal of relationships: non-comma punctuation, such as semicolons, colons, and parentheses. These latter two marks tend to be favored by less sophisticated writers, since commas potentially signal many relationships, whereas colons and parentheses signal only a few. As we might expect, then, Franklin's non-comma punctuation is restricted to colons and parentheses—the latter to punctuate his more frequently used middle-position free modifiers, which are easier to read when punctuated by parentheses than when punctuated by commas. In fact, in his entire written output (including all drafts of all proposals), Franklin uses a semicolon only once, and then incorrectly:

Management must identify viable geographic location alternatives very quickly; yet very carefully.

Baker, however, while hardly liberal in his use of semicolons, employs them in three of his four proposals.

A final aspect of punctuation as a cohesive device shows dramatically how much less of a burden Baker imposes on his readers: while Baker leaves only three percent of his free modifiers unpunctuated, Franklin leaves fully fifteen percent not set off by a punctuation mark, making it more difficult for readers to be able to recognize quickly the juncture between a free modifier and one of his relatively long independent clauses.

Graphic Cohesion. Because he makes comparatively little use of linguistic cohesive devices, Franklin makes much greater use of graphic ones. For example, he uses about 21 headings per 100 T-units (versus 14 for Baker), and he highlights structures much more freqently (27 times per 100 T-units, versus 19 times), often indenting parts of a long clause for readability:

At this point, we will prepare a summary report that describes the:
- –approach used in conducting the study
- –our basic conclusions
- –our recommendations
- –a basic implementation plan.

Of course, highlighting by splitting up a noun and the article that precedes it is rare in Franklin's writing, and he later amends this particular instance by removing "the" after "describes" and inserting it before "approach"; but even so, Franklin is much more likely to use this graphic technique to clarify the grammatical structure of a sentence, whereas Baker is more likely to use the linguistic strategy of casting the idea into a relatively short independent clause, followed by a list (free modifier) that is introduced by a colon.

Among all writers, probably the most common graphic technique is indenting for a paragraph. Baker and Franklin write paragraphs of similar length: 60 words for Baker, 53 for Franklin. However, as with T-unit length, Baker is much more flexible about paragraph length than Franklin: the standard deviation for his paragraph mean of 60 is 40, whereas the standard devation for Franklin's mean of 53 is only 29.

Style and Usage. Baker and Franklin also differ in two of three aspects of style. First, Franklin uses twice as many clausal patterns that textbooks usually characterize as being weak, wordy, or otherwise unattractive: passive-voice construction, anticipatory constructions ("there are" or "it is"), and clausal frames ("Table X shows that y is z"). In fact, more than four out of ten of Franklin's clauses are of one of these types—again, a sign of a relatively unsophisticated style. Second, Franklin is even more tolerant of many so-called errors of usage, with 24 out of 100 T-units being marked by dangling modifiers, split infinitives, colons in mid-sentence, missing commas before "and" in the last element in a series, and so on (vs. only 18 for Baker). Again, this is a sign not of bad writing, but rather of relatively unpolished writing. In a measure of "reader-interest" popularized by Rudolf Flesch, both writers use personal pronouns at about the same rate (51 per 100 T-units for Baker, 49 per 100 for Franklin).

By almost every quantifiable measure of style, then, Baker proves to be relatively more sophisticated, more polished, more elegant.

Such a remark should by no means suggest that Franklin is a bad writer, nor even an unsophisticated one. Viewed from almost any realistic perspective, he must be judged a highly effective user of language, as might be expected from the considerable success he has had as a problem solver and a proposal writer. But, relatively speaking, Baker is *more* sophisticated in his manipulation of the resources of language.

This difference in linguistic sophistication appears to be an important influence on their respective composing and revising processes, along with the importance of the project, the nature of the task, and the characteristics of clients. At root, Baker likes to play with a proposal, fussing over it almost for its own sake; Franklin likes to bang it out and be done with it.

With these differing backgrounds, concepts, and predispositions in mind, we may now turn to an analysis of Baker's and Franklin's composing/revising processes.

Analysis of the Eight Proposals

Both Baker's and Franklin's cultural and personal characteristics, including their usual methods of composing, are reflected in their eight proposals. Summary data for all eight are shown in Appendix C.3 and C.4 (which express the number of voluntary changes for each norm, process, and orientation as a percent of all voluntary changes) and in C.5 and C.6 (which break down figures for each orientation into the twenty-six goals). Since these proposals have many similar characteristics, we will avoid needless repetition by examining the first in considerable detail, first analyzing Baker's goals in Bak-A, and then tracing his draft-by-draft process in that proposal. Then we will examine the other seven proposals more briefly.

Baker's Goals in Proposal Bak-A

Baker's proposal Bak-A was addressed to an officer of an art museum. The task to be undertaken for the museum was to determine the feasibility of pulling together all of the museum's fifteen to thirty marketing functions into one unit. The Firm committed itself to 150 days of work, for a total cost of $98,000; the proposal was 3,489 words long in its final draft.

To prepare the proposal, Baker and the Firm's chairman of the board met with the museum's president and three vice-presidents and took considerable notes. Then Baker abstracted relevant information from the museum's 370-page long-range plan and from its five-page request for proposal (RFP). He also reviewed the Firm's previous experience in doing studies for not-for-profit organizations and finally met with other officers in the Firm to discuss the information he had gathered.

As a result of his personal interviews with the directors of the museum and his analysis of various documents which stated the museum's long-range goals and standing principles, Baker identified an overriding concern of his audience: an interest not merely in financial or commercial goals, but also in humanistic and artistic goals to which scholars and artists subscribe, including esthetic and intellectual values and an institutional infrastructure based on consensus. As Baker said of one interview, "They kept hitting us with . . . 'we aren't oriented to the bottom line—don't tell us how to increase volume when we want to increase quality. Make sure that you do not hurt our basic mission, threaten our basic mission. And also, we work by consensus.'" Thus, Baker isolated an important situational norm to supplement the need for a solution to the client's problem: he and the Firm had to avoid the appearance of a "bottom-line" mentality, a "profits-first" outlook that would seem insensitive to the museum's cultural role and that would thus antagonize its professional staff, whose jobs might be affected by any changes proposed by the Firm and whose cooperation would be essential to the study itself.

With this background information about Proposal Bak-A in mind, we can turn to a goal-by-goal analysis of Baker's revising process.

Goal 1: To Be Accurate. As shown in Appendix C.6, about 14 percent of Baker's voluntary revisions to Bak-A consisted of efforts to improve the accuracy of the language used to express ideas. Cultural norms led him to add, delete, or replace many words and phrases for this purpose. For example, he changed "Some information is shared or centralized" to "Some *marketing* information is shared or centralized" in order to specify the kind of information he had in mind. In another instance, he replaced the term "department heads" with the title actually used by the client ("directors"). In response to generic norms, he changed a word describing a functional section of the proposal, replacing the word "objectives" (a term which refers to the concepts relevant to the Firm's task in preparing recommendations for the client) with the word "recommendations" (the term for a standard section of a report). In response to institutional norms, he changed place-holder blanks to specific dates or dollar amounts, using information provided by the Firm. In response to personal preference, he changed "visual presentation" to "graphic presentation."

Goal 2: To Be Safe. Closely akin to the goal of accurate expression is the goal of safe expression, accomplished by qualifying or removing assertions (explicit or implicit) whose truth or falsity is problematical or which might commit Baker or the Firm to perform more than they intend to undertake. Two percent of Baker's voluntary changes to Bak-A had this goal as an aim. For example, in the first draft, he generated the following claim:

> In some areas, growth in numbers appears to be a reasonable objective. These include the income-generating functions of mail order, food service, and rights and reproductions.

Since, however, the Firm had not yet performed a detailed study of the museum, Baker qualified the assertion of the second sentence by inserting the qualifier "may": "These *may* include . . ." Similarly, he changed a commitment to "meet individually with each department head" to a commitment to "meet with each *applicable* department head". Other inserted qualifying phrases included "in some cases," "frequently," "existing," and "currently used." In another instance, Baker revised a reference to "the for-profit experiences of the Trustees" by deleting the phrase "for-profit," since he had no way of determining whether all of the museum's trustees had in fact had "for-profit" experiences. Again, these changes were made not to remove an inaccurate remark or to make a remark more accurate, but rather to qualify a claim whose accuracy could not be determined or to temper an overly exuberant or overly general remark.

Goal 3: To Be Thorough. Nine percent of Baker's changes were designed not to express an idea more clearly but rather to extend the scope of a claim or promise. Many of these were small-scale changes. For example, he changed "ideas" to "ideas and opportunities," "compensation" to "compensation and fringe benefits," and "objectives, means, and measures" to "objectives, goals, means, and measures." Such revisions for thoroughness were usually prompted by cultural, institutional, or personal norms. At times, however, such additions were prompted by situational norms—developing an idea in order to make it clear to a particular, relatively uninformed reader. For example, in his first draft, he promised to provide "concise position descriptions" for any proposed reorganization of the museum staff. Later, realizing that the museum staff might not know what is involved in a position description, he inserted a sentence to provide a brief definition: "Position descriptions will include job definition, requirements, skills and experience, objectives and responsibilities."

Goal 4: To Be Relevant. The corollary of being thorough is being relevant—that is, eliminating irrelevant information, which occurred in two percent of Baker's voluntary changes to Bak-A. On a very small scale, for example, Baker deleted the irrelevant word "measures" from the phrase "objectives, goals, means . . . , and measures." In a more extensive deletion for relevance, the following four-structure heading group was removed:

> *13. Present to Directors.* Using the objectives previously developed and presented to Directors, review the conceptual alternatives and describe the logic for selecting the recommended marketing organization and strategy approach. Provide sufficient time for questions and answers and ample discussion.

Goal 5: To Be Coherent. Between 1 and 2 percent of Baker's low-affect, idea-oriented, voluntary revisions were intended to alter the logical or rhetorical structure of the text. On two occasions, this involved moving a complete paragraph (one composed of nine structures, the other of five). But the remaining changes in this category involved only a single structure.

Goal 6: To Signal Relationships with a Cohesive Tie. Many of Baker's changes involved inserting a free modifier ("in short," "next," "however," "finally," "therefore") or a bound word or phrase ("also," "at this point," "on the following page," "thereby," "the following"). Other voluntary goal 6 changes involved pronouns (for example, changing "these" to "the," inserting "both," changing "the" to "this"). No fewer than twenty involuntary changes involved renumbering headings to accompany the insertion of a new heading group (that is, when three new steps were inserted into a description of a twelve-step activity, all of the headings for activities discussed after the insertions had to be renumbered). In all, 2 percent of Baker's voluntary changes to Bak-A were aimed at goal 6.

Goal 7: To Signal Relationships with Punctuation. Baker's voluntary revisions for this goal were of three sorts. First, he hyphenated adjectival compounds such as "easily-measurable," "short-term," "consensus-supported," "income-generation," "bottom-line," and "top-level." Second, he punctuated already existing free modifiers or coordinate clauses:

> Old: We estimate that Phase I and Phase II respectively can be completed within two-and-a-half to three months.

> New: We estimate that Phase I and Phase II, respectively, can be completed within two-and-a-half to three months.

Third, in other proposals, he punctuated the last element in a complicated series, even though such punctuation runs counter to the Firm's style guide for the word-processing unit. An example of this is found in the following complicated series, where he inserted a comma between "prices" and "and maintaining":

> You wish to secure outside forecasting assistance from a firm qualified in evaluating forecasting techniques, understanding regulatory influences, reviewing and reacting to economic trends, dealing effectively with truck producers, understanding sensitivities to fuel availability and prices, and maintaining on-going contact and involvement with the industry, its suppliers and customers.

Note that, as mentioned in chapter 3, he left unpunctuated the series within the last element of the main series: "involvement with the industry, its suppliers and customers." Two percent of Baker's voluntary revisions were for this goal.

Baker's *involuntary* goal 7 revisions occurred when, for example, a voluntary join and recasting of two structures into one needed to be accompanied by punctuation:

Old: Many of the museum's priorities and objectives don't have "growth" and "bottom line" as an objective. Any consulting assistance or marketing program must relate to these non-business priorities.

New: Where priorities don't have "growth" and "bottom line" objectives, consulting assistance must relate to non-business priorities.

(In a later revision, Baker avoided weak repetition by changing the first instance of "priorities" to "activities.") Splits and moves also frequently require such involuntary adjustment of punctuation.

In a *typographic* revision, Baker replaced a period with a comma to repair a sentence fragment:

Old: Also, because they will ultimately review and approve organizational changes. Their continuing involvement is important.

New: Also, because they will ultimately review and approve organizational changes, their continuing involvement is important.

Goal 8: To Signal Relationships by Graphic Means. About 4 percent of Baker's revisions were designed to signal relationships by means of a heading, a paragraph indentation, or highlighting (italicizing, underscoring, setting off a structure or passage with "white space").

Goal 9: To Signal Relationships through Syntax. Five percent of Baker's revisions altered syntactic parallelism, nonparallelism, or order to show the functional similarity or difference in the ideas expressed in the structures. For example, in one long list introduced by a colon, each element in the list except one was modified by a noun-phrase sentence fragment, as in the following:

Objectives. Written and assumed objectives, means to attain them, and measures.

The exceptional element in the list consisted of a verbal modifier set off by a comma:

Interviewee background, including: current position, involvement in the marketing process . . .

Therefore, he recast the exceptional element, changing it from a participial phrase to an appositive:

> *Interviewee background.* Current position, involvement in the marketing process . . .

In another revision to create linguistic echoes that signal similarity of meaning or function, Baker changed a declarative sentence into an interrogative one. He also recast a partial-form (nounless) clause ("Define objectives for marketing efforts") to a full-form pattern ("We will define objectives for marketing efforts") in order to echo a previous sentence ("We will establish reasonable ranges of compensation for each marketing position"). Other goal 9 changes joined parallel sentences into parallel T-units to emphasize the relationship between ideas:

> Old: As a cultural resource, the museum is invaluable. As an institution, the museum provides a unique diversity of functions and services.

> New: As a cultural resource, the museum is invaluable; as an institution, it provides a unique diversity of functions and services.

> Old: Some information is shared or centralized. The annual budgeting process, which is controlled by Administration, contains totals for applicable marketing activities. In addition, the membership list is shared for a large part of mailings. Finally, most scheduling is administered by Administration. Nonetheless, current marketing activities communicate separate messages and may result in extra costs because of missed synergy in shared activities.

> New: Some marketing information is shared or centralized: the annual budget allocates totals for marketing activities; the membership list is shared for most mailings; most promotional scheduling is controlled by administration. Nonetheless, marketing activities often communicate separate messages and probably cause extra costs because of duplication of effort.

In the latter example, Baker combined his account of the few instances of "centralization" into a single sentence, thus clarifying the fact that, despite the presence of five sentences in the original passage, there were really only two main ideas. As a result of his recasting the first four sentences into a base clause and a series of three repeating clauses, the sentence beginning "Nonetheless" was much more emphatic in the revised version, and thus helped Baker focus on the museum's need for the Firm's consulting assistance.

Goal 10: To Signal Relationships by Lexical Means. As we noted in chapter 1, some changes do not clarify an idea by adding more information or by using different language (as in goal 1), but rather clarify relationships between existing ideas by supplying lexical referents rather than abstract cohesive ties such as "however" or "the following." Such lexical reference is accomplished by repetition of a key term, by synonyms, or by frame sentences (for example, "The following persons were hired"). For example, in one instance, Baker inserted the word "measurable" before the word "goals" in order to make a clear backward reference to the word "measures" in a previous sentence. And in the example below, he clarified the scope of the abstract cohesive tie "the following" by adding a lexical referent:

> This experience includes organization, marketing and planning studies for the following:

> This experience includes organization, marketing, and planning studies for the following organizations.

(In a later draft, Baker again recast the sentence to avoid the weak repetition of "organizations.")

In addition to changes for forward reference (cataphoric cohesion), Baker also made changes for backward reference (anaphoric cohesion). For example, at one point he decided to change an independent clause into an absolute clause; as he did so, he added the word "function" to improve the backward reference of "each":

> Old: . . . each utilizes its own information, approach, and independent design and support services.

> New: . . . with each function utilizing its own information, approach, and independent design and support services.

In all, about four percent of Baker's voluntary revisions were for goal 10.

Goal 11: To Be Readable. Nearly 3 percent of Baker's revisions to Bak-A were intended to make the text easier to read and comprehend by combining, breaking up, or otherwise recasting difficult-to-understand structures. These changes are distinct from goal 7 revisions, which merely punctuate an existing structure, as in the following:

> Old: Objectives of separate organizational units are not entirely similar nor are they necessarily compatible in all cases.

> New: Objectives of separate organizational units are not entirely similar, nor are they necessarily compatible in all cases.

In yet other instances, a more thorough-going recasting was required, especially when a single structure was broken into two or more structures:

> Old: . . . it would be developed in such a way to assure that priorities and values of the museum would be internalized and that the marketing function would operate as a coordinator and a service rather than as an antagonist.

> New: . . . it would be designed to assure that basic priorities and values of the museum would be maintained, so that marketing will operate as a coordinator and a service, rather than as an antagonist.

In other cases, structures that contained multiply embedded relative clauses or infinitive phrases were recast for readability:

> Old: It is the only major museum which has a school which offers degree programs.

> New: It is the only major museum with a school offering degree programs.

> Old: It is the objective of this study to resolve the complex organization and marketing issues to assure that the museum effectively support both its qualitative and quantitative needs.

New: This study will resolve the complex organization and marketing issues and assure that the museum effectively provide marketing support to achieve its qualitative and quantitative goals.

Goal 12: To Condense. Next to accuracy, conciseness was Baker's
most frequently addressed goal: 14 percent of his revisions eliminated wordiness. In many cases, he eliminated redundancy, as in
changing "experts in specialized areas" to "experts," since an expert
by definition has an area of specialization. For the same reason, he
removed "applicable" from "applicable marketing activities," since
the context made it clear that only applicable activities were being
discussed. Elsewhere, he changed nominalized phrases to verbs:

Old: take great care to avoid
New: avoid

Old: would be developed in such a way to assure
New: would be designed to assure

Old: should provide a true reflection of
New: should reflect

Old: in a way that is supportive of the museum
New: to support the museum

Old: assure the museum of obtaining the most effective marketing orga-
    nization in terms of supporting
New: assure that the museum effectively support

Old: techniques as a basis for the development of a plan
New: techniques to develop a plan

Goal 13: To Avoid Weak Repetition. About 3 percent of Baker's
revisions were aimed at eliminating redundancy or ineffective repetition. For example, he changed "administered" to "controlled" to
avoid the redundant "administered by Administration." Elsewhere,
he changed "For example, for some areas . . ." to "For example, in
some areas . . ."

Goal 14: To Sound Better. Three percent of his revisions created

euphonious or personally desirable phrasing, as in eliminating unintentional chimes of affixes ("measuring marketing"). Often these
might be considered goal 16 revisions (to use idiomatic or conventional phrasing), except that he replaced an idiomatic phrase with
another, as in changing "cause" to "result in," "concern about" to
"concern over," or the odd "similar format to" to the equally odd
"similar format as."

Goal 15: To Spell Correctly. None of Baker's voluntary changes
altered spelling for the better; in every correction of spelling, the
change repaired a typographic error by the person operating the
Firm's word processor, and thus was classified as an involuntary
change.

Goal 16: To Use Idiomatic or Conventional Phrasing. About 3
percent of Baker's revisions made expressions more idiomatic. Usually these involved prepositions. For example, he changed "for marketing organization" to "for the marketing organization"; "relevant
in" to "relevant to"; "assistance for" to "assistance in"; "synergy in
activities" to "synergy from activities"; "described in format" to "described in a format"; "goals for XXX" to "goals of XXX"; and "observations for how to" to "observations on how to."

Goal 17: To Capitalize Letters Correctly. Less than 1 percent of
his voluntary revisions involved typographic cases, as in changing
"city of Los Angeles" to "City of Los Angeles." However, a substantial number of involuntary changes were guided by this goal in order
to accompany voluntary splits and joins.

Goal 18: To Observe Usage. About 1 percent of his revisions addressed matters such as split infinitives, dangling modifiers, contractions, use of "none" as a plural, use of apostrophes, and the like.
Unless clarity was at issue, he felt little compunction to address
such handbook concerns. Despite the presence of several split infinitives, he eliminated only a couple of them; his other goal 18 revisions involved the "rule of ten"—as in changing a numeral ("9") to a
word ("nine").

Goal 19: To Punctuate Correctly. Less than 0.5 of one percent of
Baker's revisions improved noncohesive punctuation (that is, marks
that did not play a significant role in the cohesive system of the
text). Indeed, he was largely indifferent to correcting such "deviant"
practices (according to many college handbooks) as using a colon in

the middle of a clause, setting off the last element in a series with a comma, or removing an unnecessary comma after the phrase "such as" or after a conjunction that opens a sentence ("But, he went home"), and the like.

Goal 20: To Achieve Grammatical Agreement or Conventional Syntax. Occasionally, Baker made a minor agreement error (for example, "criteria which has been established," "these effort"); about 1 percent of his voluntary changes remedied such gaffes. But for the most part, his goal 20 revisions were involuntary changes to accompany splits, joins, and moves.

This is illustrated most simply by his change of "are" to "is" to accompany the deletion of "volumes, and other quantitative data" in the following example:

> Old: Growth, volumes, and other quantitative data are not necessarily relevant for several museum objectives.

> New: Growth is not necessarily meaningful for museum objectives.

In other cases, involuntary goal 20 changes consisted of duplicative codings to specify how a join, move, or split was accomplished. For example, in a passage already cited, Baker joined two sentences. He did so by deleting a structure ("Generally"), by inserting "with," and by replacing "utilizes" with "utilizing" in order to change the independent clause into an absolute:

> Old: The museum performs marketing activities in the . . . restaurant operations, special events, and publications departments. Generally, each function utilizes its own information, approach, and independent design and support services.

> New: The museum performs marketing activities in the . . . restaurant operations, special events, and publications departments, with each function utilizing its own information, approach, and independent design and support services.

In our system of coding, the join was classified as a voluntary revision, while the deletion, insertion, and replacement were all considered involuntary changes. In other words, the term "join" is a summary or generalization whose meaning consists of the deletion, insertion, and replacement taken as a whole. Thus, the terms *delete*, *insert*, and *replace* may be said to "duplicate" the term *join* in this case, since the acts which they denote constitute the primary or voluntary act of joining.

Goal 21: To Avoid a Threat. About 7 percent of Baker's revisions were intended to remove a claim or implication that might have threatened the position or well-being of the reader. As we noted earlier, Baker's initial analysis had isolated two potential threats to his reader: first, a "bottom-line" approach to the museum's goals; second, a top-down rather than a consensus-oriented approach to management and decision making. Both threats were frequently addressed in his revisions. For example, he addressed this problem in his very first draft:

> Growth, volumes, and other quantitative data are not necessarily relevant for several museum objectives.

But to reduce the "bottom-line" threat even more, he later inserted the qualifier "pure" and deleted the qualifier "several" (which suggested that other objectives *were* oriented toward the bottom line):

> Pure growth is not necessarily meaningful for museum objectives.

For the same reason, he elsewhere inserted "in numbers," deleted "and profitable," and replaced "strategy" with "objective" in a passage dealing with financial changes that might be addressed in the future:

> Old: In some areas, growth appears to be a reasonable and profitable strategy.

> New: In some areas, growth in numbers appears to be a reasonable objective.

In another place, he first wrote the positive-sounding "Certainly, aggressive growth and 'profitability' improvement are required strategies for these areas." Later, he changed "certainly" to "seemingly" and "required" to "reasonable" so that the threat of a bottom-line orientation was considerably reduced. To show the Firm's awareness of the museum's commitment to management by consensus, his first draft assured the reader that his plan to alter the management of marketing programs would be accomplished without a monolithic organizational structure:

> It may be that the best potential could be simply in providing the forum for communication and negotiation.

Later, to emphasize this theme of nonauthoritarian consensus (implied by "forum for communication and negotiation"), he recast the sentence as follows:

> A viable alternative might simply be to provide a forum for communication and negotiation without centralizing authority.

Other threats that arose during the composing process were also dealt with. For example, as he explained what gave rise to the museum's request for a proposal from the Firm, Baker first wrote the following:

> Recently, the museum's chairman of the board . . . has recommended that significant opportunities exist for cost reduction, operating synergy, and message consistency through the closer coordination of marketing. . . .

Later, Baker felt this passage might imply too great a commitment by the chairman to this project. After all, one of the main purposes of Baker's proposed study was to determine whether "significant opportunities" actually existed. If the study was negative—that is, if it turned out there were no money-saving results forthcoming—then the passage would have sounded as if the chairman had made a wrong prediction, and a costly one at that. To reduce this threat to the chairman's reputation for good judgment, Baker replaced "has recommended" with "suggested" and inserted the qualifiers "may" before "exist," and "improved" before "consistency." Now, the chairman no longer appeared to be making a rash promise, but instead appeared to be offering a reasonable prediction:

Recently, the museum's chairman of the board . . . suggested that opportunities may exist for cost reduction, operating synergy, and improved message consistency through closer coordination of marketing. . . .

Goal 22: To Avoid an Insult. Another 4 percent of Baker's changes were intended to remove a claim or implication that might ridicule or insult the reader. For example, in his first draft, he noted that the museum's trustees had "participated directly in many of the important issues affecting the study." Later, he realized that "many" implied "not all," so that in effect he was saying that the trustees were not involved in all of the museum's important decisions. To avoid this implicit insult, he deleted "many of the" in a later draft. Similarly, in referring to museum personnel, he first wrote that "most of the staff is comprised of . . . experts"; to avoid the insulting implication that some of its staff were *not* experts, he deleted the qualifying phrase "most of." In another place, he noted that his plan would address a problem related to personnel: "How will the individuals within the structure work together?" Later, to avoid the implication that museum staff might have difficulty working with one another, he changed the person-oriented word "individuals" to the more abstract term "positions"—a word that was not only more accurate, but also less insulting.

Goal 23: To Bond with the Reader. Not quite 1 percent of Baker's revisions were designed to establish rapport between the writer and the reader. Most of these occurred when he was emphasizing the need for consensus—not only among museum personnel, but also between museum personnel and the consultants from the Firm. One such revision consisted of a generalization added to emphasize the intended interplay between client and consultant staffs: "Consensus comes from discussion, negotiation and confidence." Another change was intended to humanize client-consultant relationships by replacing the abstract connective "furthermore" with the more personal, client-including phrase "as we proceed." Another change emphasized the writer's personal involvement by setting off a coordinate clause with a comma:

Old: I will have the overall responsibility for the study and I commit to participating actively in the work.

New: I will have the overall responsibility for the study, and I commit to
participating actively in the work.

If we had not been able to interview Baker, of course, we would
have classified this last change as a low-affect revision for goal 7 (to
signal relationships by means of punctuation).
Goal 24: To Build Credit. Over 8 percent of Baker's revisions
added claims or implications about "his" attributes (that is, those of
the Firm's chair, for whom he was ghost-writing the proposal) or his
firm's attributes that would impress the reader (or that would eliminate self-damaging claims or implications). Many of these revisions
dealt with the Firm's capacity for helping the museum (showing that
it was ready, willing, and able to do so). For example, at one point
Baker condensed the text (changing a wordy frame to a concise, first-
person, active voice) in order to achieve a more positive tone about
the Firm's abilities:

Old: From these resources, it will be our intention to help the museum
develop a means to effectively coordinate and improve its marketing
activities.

New: Using these sources, we will help the museum develop a means to
effectively coordinate and improve its marketing activities.

In yet a later draft, he returned to the same passage in order to highlight the Firm's abilities even further by starting the sentence with
the phrase "Using these sources and our management perspective
. . ." Elsewhere, he changed a low-affect reference to the Firm's
staff ("they") with a phrase that suggested more positive characteristics ("our team"). In another place, he inserted credit-building information about the Firm relevant to the client's desire for goals
other than commercial gain (the bottom line): "The Firm has extensive experience working for not-for-profit organizations throughout
North America and abroad." Along the same lines, he supported an
initial credit-building claim about the Firm ("we guarantee that the
study will achieve the results described in this proposal") with an
even more positive-sounding claim: ". . . and we will undertake at
our cost whatever additional effort is required to achieve the highest
professional standards of performance." And in another revision, he

changed "we plan to use a team of senior professionals" to the even more creditable (though semantically questionable) "we plan to use a team of very senior professionals."

Goal 25: To Create or Feed a Wish. In about 7 percent of his revisions, Baker added claims or implications that stressed positive results for the reader or that created or satisfied a need in the reader. Often, these revisions were prompted by generic requirements to establish a need for change—that is, to confirm the reader's concern about the status quo and hence the belief that consulting assistance was needed. For example, in an early draft, he buttressed his claim that there was a need for action with a supporting remark by the client's chairman of the board:

> The museum's chairman . . . has suggested that opportunities may exist for cost reduction, operating synergy, and improved message consistency through closer coordination of marketing.

Later, he recast this claim to focus not only on the need for change but also on the need for consulting assistance:

> The museum's chairman . . . has suggested the need for profound and objective counsel to assist the museum to identify what opportunities may exist for improved communications, operating synergy, as well as more cost effective marketing programs throughout the museum.

And having recast the text for this new emphasis, he moved it from its original position in the middle of the problem section to a more prominent position near the end, where it could do the most good in influencing the client's management to accept the need for action and the need for consulting assistance—acceptance sought by the writer as a necessary psychological step toward the client's granting the Firm a contract. Similarly, at the very end of the problem section, just before he began to explain what the Firm's proposed study would accomplish, he first set up the new section with a summary statement:

> It is the objective of this study to resolve that and other issues and to assure the museum of obtaining the most effective marketing organiza-

tion in terms of supporting both the qualitative and quantitative needs of the museum.

Later, he both condensed this statement and fed the reader's wish for change by returning to his "complexity" theme in a recasting of the summary statement:

> This study will resolve the complex organization and marketing issues and assure that the museum effectively provide marketing support to achieve both its qualitative and quantitative goals.

Other changes were intended to "decenter" the text—to move from a focus on his task as a proposal writer or the Firm's task as a consulting source to the client's concern with its own problems. To give only two examples of many, we may first examine his revision of the following sentence:

> Should a centralized group approach be advisable, it would be developed in such a way to assure that priorities and values of the museum would be internalized and that the marketing function would operate as a coordinator and a service rather than as an antagonist.

In revising this sentence, Baker had many goals in mind, but one important one was to get rid of his "writer-based" concern with "internalizing" the goals of the museum. This was writer-based because it focused on his task (and the Firm's), rather than on his reader's wishes. The revision, among other things, moved toward a "reader-based" focus by eliminating the idea of internalizing values (which, of course, the client had already internalized):

> Should a centralized group approach be advisable, it would be designed to assure that basic priorities and values of the museum would be maintained; that marketing be a coordinator and a service, not an antagonist.

More subtly, he decentered one remark by changing a promise to answer one question ("Where will the report fit in the organization?") to a promise to answer another—one more clearly relevant to the client's wish for a more efficient organization: "Where will marketing fit in the organization?"

In yet other cases, the revisions simply altered the tone to establish a mood of positive results, as when he replaced the abstract linking expression "such a result" with a phrase that clearly expressed the desires of the client: "bringing together the various marketing activities." Elsewhere, having first written that "we are impressed with the atmosphere which you provide," he played to his client's wishes by adding a goal-oriented phrase: "We are impressed with the atmosphere which you provide for a successful study."

Goal 26: To Stroke the Reader. Not quite 1 percent of Baker's revisions were intended to add claims or implications that would commend or flatter the reader. For example, he first referred to the museum staff as "experts," but then changed that to the more flattering "creative experts." He first wrote that the Firm was sensitive to "not-for-profit organizations," but then changed that to "not-for-profit organizations in a professional environment like the museum." He first wrote that the "knowledge and experience of the senior management of the museum will provide an important foundation for the study," but then upgraded the senior management's status (and their sense of their status) by saying they would provide "*the* foundation" for the study (our italics).

Baker's Draft-By-Draft Process in Bak-A

The analysis of Baker's goals, of course, tells only half the story. Equally important is the process by which he implemented these changes as he worked his way through the proposals draft by draft. Before describing that process, however, we must first discuss two matters: first, our partitioning of the proposals into three functional sections; second, our definition of the ambiguous word "draft."

At the Firm, proposals generally consist of three major sections: problem, methods, and implementation. From the perspective of the text, these are distinguishable by differences in mode; from the perspective of the writing situation, they are distinguishable by differences in rhetorical function; and, as we will note later, from the perspective of the writing process, they are distinguishable by the fact that both writers in our study often created the first draft of a proposal not in one composing session but in several, and each session wais generally devoted to just one of the three main sections.

As explained in chapter 3, the problem section usually consists of a brief introduction (salutation and statement of the letter's purpose), an analysis of the client's problems, and an overview of the kind of solution required in the client's particular case. It describes not only a general need for a solution to the problem, but also a specific need for the firm's consulting assistance in finding a solution. In generic terms, it consists of parts often called "background," "objectives," and "study strategy." The methods section consists of a detailed exposition of the steps that the firm would follow in providing the consulting assistance that would solve the client's problem. It is sometimes called the "approach" section. The implementation section consists of a part on the cost for the consulting work, a part on the staff to be used (sometimes with an additional "qualifications" part), and a conclusion voicing the writer's confidence that the work would be successful. Thus, in terms of mode (as we use the term), the problem section is mainly argument, the methods section is mainly exposition, and the implementation section is partly exposition and partly argument.

In terms of rhetorical function or aim, the problem section has to describe the problem and need so effectively that the client will be confirmed in his or her preexisting belief in a problem and will be confident that the writer understands the problem. The methods section has to describe a specific means of achieving a solution which will seem appropriate to the problem and which will be detailed enough to show that the writer knows more than the client about the means of finding a solution. The implementation section has to provide a businesslike estimate of monetary costs; it also has to describe the Firm's staff in such a way that they will appear capable of solving the problem and will seem agreeable to the client (who will have to work with them). In addition, the implementation section has to help the client "visualize" the potential benefits of consulting assistance. In sum, the three sections of the Firm's proposals clearly have different, genre-imposed rhetorical functions or aims.

Besides partitioning the proposals into functional units, we have also had to deal with the problematic concept of a "draft." Because both Baker and Franklin sometimes displayed an asymmetrical pattern of generating and revising their proposals, the term "draft" can be quite ambiguous: from one point of view, it could be synonymous with "typescript"; from another point of view, it could be synonymous with "session of generating or revising," so that a writer might produce two "drafts" on one typescript.

To achieve some regularity of analysis, we have stipulated that the "first draft" consists of the first, unrevised text of at least the first two of the three sections, whether or not they used preexisting material (either boilerplate or original text by a second, subordinate author) and whether or not they were all generated in one session of composing or were each written in a different session. We have further stipulated that any subsequent "draft" must include revisions of at least two of the three sections on any typescript; if only one section is revised, we term those revisions a "run-through" rather than a draft, and we include such revisions in the totals for subsequent revisions of the entire draft. At the same time, we have calculated statistical information for every draft and every run-through of each section of all eight proposals, since both Baker and Franklin appeared to revise different sections in different ways and for different purposes. These stipulations hold for all eight proposals, not just for Bak-A.

As noted earlier, Baker's first steps toward writing down a draft consisted of notes that he took during an interview with museum personnel and while reading relevant museum documents. After studying these notes, he rearranged them and others made during the study period, cutting and pasting them into a rough line of thought. He then dictated the problem section, a six-page (double-spaced) typewritten statement of the museum's problems and needs. While that section was being typed up by the Firm's word-processing unit, he dictated the methods section. Then, while the dictation tape of the methods section was at the word-processing unit, he made an initial run-through of handwritten revisions (in green ink) to the problem section. As shown in Appendix C.7 (where this run-through is labeled draft 2a), slightly less than half (43 of 94 per 100) of this first batch of revisions addressed ideas or high affect, with the remaining changes giving descending attention to style, cohesion, and usage, respectively. As a result, T-unit length dipped very slightly (from 18.0 to 17.8), independent clause length slightly more so (from 16.4 to 15.6). The emphasis on cohesion was reflected in sharp jumps in the rate of cohesive ties and headings. Also, the usage-error rate dropped from 26 to 20.

Baker next dictated the implementation section. When both the methods and the implementation sections were returned from the word-processing unit, he made a revising run-through of all three sections, adding the changes by hand in red ink (so that the type-script of the problem section had two sets of marks, one in green and one in red, while the methods and implementations sections had only one set of marks, in red). In the second run-through of the problem section, Baker's revision rate climbed from 94 for the green-ink changes to 155 for the red-ink changes. High-affect and usage rates remained about even, the cohesion rate dropped by nearly 50 percent, and the idea rate climbed threefold, from 9 to 28. But the most dramatic change was in the style rate, which rose from 24 to a remarkable 77—the highest style rate by either writer in any draft of any proposal. Almost all of these style changes were devoted to goal 12, conciseness. This disparate focus on conciseness resulted partly from the fact that Baker revised the section twice and partly from his wish to avoid using typical consultant's jargon, which is sometimes wordy, and which he felt was inappropriate for this client. The results of this extraordinary pattern on the text were equally remarkable. The T-unit mean, which had dipped slightly from 18.0 to 17.8 in the first run-through, fell to 15.7; and the independent clause mean fell from 16.4 in the first draft and 15.6 in the first run-through to 13.6, so that, mainly as a result of his revising for conciseness, the T-unit mean fell 2.3 words during the first two run-throughs. At the same time, several cohesion-oriented splits reduced the paragraph mean from 57 to 42 words, so that the "look" of the pages seemed a little cleaner, more attractive, and more appropriate for a proposal in letter format. The general effect of these changes, therefore, was to improve the readability of the text considerably.

As he turned to the methods section, however, his voluntary rate was only 119 (vs. 155 in the problem section), and his attention to the various orientations became more balanced, though more than half were still devoted to idea (46) or high affect (17). In many of these idea changes, he added new elements in lists of activities that

the Firm would perform; this increased the percent of words in
final-position free modifiers (from 18 to 25). Finally, the usage rate
of 17 caused the usage error rate to drop from 25 to 15.

His first set of changes to the implementation section echoed his
approach to the second run-through of the problem section (column
2b in Appendix C.7), except for a more balanced attention to style. In
his high-affect revisions to the implementation section, he fleshed
out descriptions of the Firm's proposed staff for this project in order
to build credit (goal 24).

When all of these changes were made by the word-processing
unit, the result was a fresh typescript, draft 2 (shown as 2b in Appendix C.7). Then, in revising the problem part of this typescript to
create draft 3, Baker continued to mark at a high rate (140), with
about 70 percent of his changes oriented toward idea or high affect;
in fact, nearly half of the changes (46 percent) were devoted to high
affect alone. As he made these changes, most of which involved insertions or replacements that increased the size of the text, T-unit
and independent clause means began to creep upward from 15.7 and
13.6 in draft 2 to 18.1 and 14.9. However, Baker took care to preserve the virtues of short independent clauses as much as possible,
adding much information by means of insertions of (and insertions
in) final-position free modifiers, so that the percentage of words in
final-position FMs rose sharply from 3 to 9. His concern with ideas
and attitudes was paralleled by some continuing attention to usage
(rate of 6), which caused a decline in the usage error rate to 20.

Interestingly, the T-unit mean in this set of revisions was nearly
the same as that of draft 1, since it rose to 18.1. But, of course, the
prose was not "unchanged." While the T-unit mean in draft 3 was
very similar to that of draft 1 (18.1 vs. 18.0), the independent clause
mean in draft 3 was only 14.9, compared to 16.4 in draft 1. Hence,
draft 3 was much more readable, since it had shorter independent
clauses, as well as greater segmentation of the text by means of free
modifiers and grammatical subordination. In other words, the potentially misleading similarity of T-unit lengths in drafts 1 and 3
demonstrates the advantage of examining both process (the seven
variables) and product (the quantifiable descriptors) when studying
writers' revisions, for the two perspectives help us identify a revising process for the problem section of Bak-A with relatively clear
stages: (a) in draft 1, generating ideas; (b) in the first run-through of

draft 2, modifying ideas, with strong secondary attention to signaling the line of thought and improving style; (c) in the second run-through of draft 2, primary emphasis on style (conciseness), with strong secondary emphasis on idea and high affect; (d) in draft 3, a renewed primary emphasis on ideas—especially by modifying the tone or affective impact of the basic concepts and the line of thought.

In producing draft 3 of the methods part, Baker increased his rate of voluntary revisions to 147 (from 119 for that section in draft 2); but two-thirds of these changes were oriented toward idea or high affect, so that, with the exception of slight decreases in T-unit and paragraph means, the quantifiable aspects of the text were not greatly altered. The same may be said for the implementation part, where 90 percent of the changes were idea or high affect. However, because new information was added to that small part of the text in the form of a few sentences composed only of relatively long independent clauses, the means for independent clauses and paragraphs rose slightly, while all other measures decreased slightly.

Draft 3 concluded Baker's active involvement in the writing of Proposal Bak-A. However, that draft was sent to a second author in the Firm, who made a final round of revisions; data about these changes have been shown as draft 4 in Appendix C.7, but have not been included in the totals column. As table C.7 shows, these revisions consisted of relatively few changes (voluntary rates of only 21, 15, and 46 respectively in the three parts). Most of them were minor adjustments whose function was less to alter the text substantively than to allow the second author to contribute in an active way to the writing of a letter that would go out under his own signature. Unfortunately, as a result of the second author's tinkering, the usage error rate rose back nearly to the rate of draft 1.

With this detailed analysis of Bak-A in mind, we may now turn to the other seven proposals.

Proposal Bak-B
Proposal Bak-B, written to a major U.S. truck machinery manufacturer, proposed a two-phase study. Phase I would last two months and cost over $200,000 (plus expenses); phase II, requiring less time, would cost about $75,000 (plus expenses). In its final version, Proposal Bak-B was 3,872 words long.

The Firm was bidding against several other consulting companies, including two of its major competitors. The situation was further complicated because of the previous relationship between Baker and the client's vice-president of planning. This person had worked for Baker when both were at a different consulting company. In this new situation, their roles would be different: now Baker hoped to work for someone who used to be his subordinate. "In our first meeting," Baker recalls, "I hadn't seen him in a few years, and I was very, very businesslike with him. I also didn't want to oversell myself. He knew my background and he knew what I could do and if I really embellished anything it would hurt, and further than that he worked with me on the major similar studies that I did in the past" at the previous consulting company. Therefore, "he was familiar with the clever things I'd try to do to sell business. I did not want him to think that I had dusted off an old proposal. I did not want him to think that I was trying to con him. I did not want him to think that I was taking advantage of our friendship."

During their meeting, Baker detected some of the major issues or hot buttons. The machinery manufacturer was greatly concerned about its credibility with its lenders because its sales forecasts had been much too high in the past. Even when it became much more conservative in its forecasting, the bottom fell out of the industry, and its forecasts were again too high. Thus, the company wanted a consulting company with considerable experience related to the proposed study. It did not want a junior team assigned, and it did want an extensive workplan, specifically detailing how the consultants would produce the study's results. And because it was possible that the Firm would have to present its results to the machinery company's lenders as well, objectivity was the key: the Firm had to establish its credibility so that the lenders would be assured that the proposed study's forecasts were indeed accurate.

Responding to these issues, Baker decided that his proposal's most important themes had to revolve around his team's considerable experience, objectivity, and commitment to the project, and this decision defined much of the proposal's content. For example, in each of the proposal's critical worksteps, Baker included a sentence such as "This step will be conducted under the direction of Jim Smith, who developed a similar econometric model in a study for Acme Machinery Company last year." In addition, Baker appended an extensive qualifications section, originally pulled together and developed by one of the Firm's senior vice-presidents. As suggested in chapter 3, an extensive and appended qualifications section is more characteristic of a government than a commercial-sector proposal. Our analysis of Baker's proposal does not include this section.

There was yet one more confounding factor facing Baker in proposal Bak-B: a tight deadline. Baker's first meeting with his old friend took place on a Thursday, and the proposal had to be presented by the following Wednesday. Because of the highly competitive situation, the proposal had to be top-flight, but Baker would not be able to present it. Moreover, the proposal had to go not only to Baker's friend, but also to his friend's boss (the corporate vice-president of planning) and the company's president. These latter two individuals Baker had never met and would not get a chance to meet. Worse, the Firm's major competitor was then doing another study for the manufacturer and thus had more access to the principal decision makers. Baker's response was to write up a number of worksteps related to some of the major issues and to meet with his friend on Monday to discuss those issues and plans. In that meeting, Baker handed his friend

> . . . a list of the information that we would require. This was intended to do two things: see if they were overwhelmed by what we needed and convince them that we were really very serious about the work. It was an extremely exhaustive list and the beauty was that they started collecting information for us before they even made up their minds. . . . Finally, we had the criteria in there for them to follow, such as what direction they should take to have maximum market possibilities. And we learned that what was really most important was maximum cash flow. And we used that in the proposal, thus making us more specifically responsive to what they wanted.

By Tuesday, Baker had what *he* wanted, and he wrote his winning proposal that afternoon. Using a four-hundred-word draft of part of the methods section (written by a colleague) and his own notes (from the meeting with the client and from his reading of the client's request for proposal), Baker dictated the problem section and most of the methods section. Since this output met our stipulated definition, we treated it as draft 1 of proposal Bak-B—a draft which for

Baker was remarkably dense, particularly in the problem section, where he produced his highest-ever first-draft T-unit and independent clause means (25.7, 17.3), percentage of weak clauses (35), and (most strikingly) usage error rate (70).

Baker produced draft 2 by revising the typescript of the problem and methods sections in one session. As with proposal Bak-A, however, he again revised the two sections differently. In the problem section, his voluntary rate (304) was the highest of either author in any draft of any section—largely because of a very high idea rate (143), accompanied by high style and cohesion rates (83 and 39, respectively), as shown in Appendix C.8. Yet, despite all of this activity, only 13 of every 100 changes involved a unit larger than a sentence; in fact, only *one* of the idea changes involved a unit of more than one grammatical structure—and that was the move of a five-structure unit. As is common in Baker's revising, the effect of his conciseness-oriented deletions was largely masked by the effect of his idea- and high-affect-oriented insertions: despite a high style rate of 83, the even higher combined rate of idea and high affect (169) cause the T-unit rates to rise sharply from 25.7 to 28.3; but, significantly, readability was not much damaged, since the base clause mean increased only slightly, from 17.3 to 17.7. Many ideas were developed by inserting information into final-position free modifiers (mainly lists of problems, needs, and previous activities), so that the T-unit mean and the percent of words in final-position free modifiers increased. In addition, the rate of usage errors dropped sharply, from 70 to 48. This at first seems odd, given the relatively small usage change rate of 13; but this seeming contradiction is a result of our methodological distinction between voluntary and nonvoluntary revisions. Many of the usage errors in draft 1 had been produced by an inept typist in the word-processing unit. Since we code the correction of typos as a type of nonvoluntary revision, Baker's extraordinary activity in this usually minor task is not evident in the data about voluntary revisions, but is clearly reflected in his rate for nonvoluntary usage changes, which was a high 35 in this draft.

In the methods section of draft 2, Baker's voluntary rate was 186 (compared to 304 in the problem section)—still a relatively high rate. But while the idea change rate was considerably lower than that of the problem section (48 vs. 143), and while the rate of changes greater than a sentence was also lower (5 vs. 13), three idea changes had a disproportionately great effect on the text, since they involved insertions of three-structure and twelve-structure passages and a move of a five-structure passage. Also, the rates for ties and headings decreased, despite a very high cohesion rate of 74. This occurred because most of Baker's cohesion changes in this section did not involve ties; instead, they focused on other goals. For example, twelve of them were designed to signal relationships by means of echoing structures, changing a series of minor-form sentences (for example, "Review activities") to major-form (for example, "We will review activities"). In another thirteen changes, Baker supplemented his original headings with a series of descriptions of proposed activities. In draft 1, the headings were merely numerals (for example, "1"); but in draft 2, these numerals were supplemented with lexical information (for example, "1. Kickoff Meeting"). Thus, despite a good deal of cohesion-oriented activity, much of which had a significant effect on the text, the ties and headings rates actually decreased because of the insertion of new T-units. However, the rate of echoes per T-unit (a measure which we are not normally reporting in this study) did increase, so Baker's attention to cohesion did result in quantifiable changes in the text. Finally, as in the problem section, the usage error rate declined sharply (from 31 to 11), despite a low rate of usage revisions. Again, this was due to efforts to repair typos.

While these changes to the problem and methods sections were being incorporated into a fresh typescript, Baker dictated two more pages for the methods section, a six-page passage about qualifications for the implementation section (three pages of which were boilerplated from company personnel files), and a two-page passage on timing and costs (boilerplated from a proposal to another client written six months earlier). When this new material returned from the word-processing unit, Baker combined the draft 2 typescript of the problem and methods sections with the new typescript of the implementation section. With this version of the entire proposal now before him, he revised each section in one session, thereby producing draft 3.

In his approach to the problem section in draft 3, Baker continued at a rather high rate of voluntary changes (182), half of which dealt with idea or high-affect changes. But while one-fourth of his draft 3 revisions to the problem section were oriented to cohesion and style (30, 13), this activity did not account for the drop in T-unit or independent clause means, since he devoted only one change to segmentation and one to conciseness in this session. Rather, the substantial drops (from 28.3 to 24.7, and from 17.7 to 15.1) were an unintentional by-product of changes made for other reasons. First, Baker decided at this time to change the format of the proposal from a pure letter to a letter-plus form. To do so, he not only inserted a title after the introduction; he also inserted a few short sentences to provide a complimentary close to what was now a short letter, rather than a salutation and introduction. Second, in the letter, Baker also inserted a short sentence to forecast (refer to) the important qualifications passage, since he knew that the Firm's qualifications were of great interest to the client. (This high-affect change would otherwise be oriented toward cohesion.) Finally, in the problem section proper, he inserted an eight-structure paragraph giving an overview of the Firm's strengths in the field to be studied. As it happened, these three changes together increased the number of T-units in the section from 23 to 33, and each change consisted of sentences with relatively short T-units and especially short independent clauses. Thus, while the quantitative data suggest that editing for conciseness had occurred, nothing of the sort had taken place; the changes were mere by-products of revisions made with other goals in mind.

In the methods section, the voluntary rate fell sharply to 34 (from 186 in draft 2 for that section). These revisions consisted mainly of minor idea changes that had little effect on the quantifiable descriptors.

In the implementation section, Baker's voluntary rate increased to 118 (since this was his first set of revisions to that section). His balanced attention to all orientations except usage produced results which did not alter the measures of quantifiable aspects of style. Still, several revisions had a great effect upon the sense or rhetorical impact of the text, since they involved changing irrelevant material in the boilerplated passages into client-specific material—most obviously, by changing a reference to the previous client by name to a reference to the current client. Several other high-affect changes involved emphasizing key phrases about the Firm's expertise (with italics) and inserting more information about the proposed staff for the study. That concluded Baker's draft 3 revisions.

Perhaps as a result of his major recasting of the proposal from pure letter to letter-plus format, Baker revised the text slightly one more time, despite the tight deadline. While he did some correcting for idea in draft 4, his main focus in all three sections was on minor adjustments oriented to cohesion and usage.

Proposal Bak-C

Unlike proposal Bak-B, Bak-C was not a competitive situation. Baker had been trying for about four years to secure business with this potential client, a leader in the building-materials industry, so when they finally did need a study done, Baker was the one called in first. And he was the only one called, apparently because Baker convinced the company president that the Firm "wouldn't scare the daylights out of" the divisional president with whom Baker would be working.

The company's president was a dynamic, aggressive, slick Harvard graduate. Although the proposal was addressed to him, the primary decision maker was a vice-president in charge of one of the divisions. Unlike the president, the vice-president was not at all polished. He had worked in the mills all his life, he was practical and direct, he did not wear a jacket to work, and he did roll up his shirtsleeves. The decision was the vice-president's because the company was "totally decentralized." The president had told Baker that if the vice-president said yes, he would say yes (though the vice-president did not know that). Thus, Baker needed to write a proposal responding to the vice-president's practical sensibilities, but he also wanted the document to be responsive to the slick-minded president, who had never before seen Baker's work and whom Baker wanted to impress for whatever future business might be in store.

To respond to the vice-president's needs, Baker used a lot of straight talk, telling him what specific deliverables he would have at the end of the study and how the resulting cost savings would end up paying for the project. Thus, unlike proposal Bak-A, written to the art museum, Baker expressed a strong bottom-line orientation: "The proposal, almost by its nature, had to have some boring recapitulation of data that really is not even relevant to the study such as costs and numbers of workers and how big the plant is and how they were organized over the years." Moreover, Baker used headings such as "Sales Effectiveness," "Customer Service," and "Organizational Effectiveness" rather than generic headings such as

"Background" or "Methods." He did not "want to sound like a heavy consultant," but rather wanted to place himself in a "sort-of-good-ol'-boy kind of role." In addition, since the vice-president was a Southerner whose plant was located in a small deep-South town, Baker brought with him to the meetings a highly experienced colleague who spoke with a strong Southern accent.

The proposal itself was designed to lay out a record of what had been discussed at the meeting and, in particular, to outline the Firm's plan for phase I, which would take thirteen weeks to complete, at a cost of about $90,000 (plus expenses). In its final version, proposal Bak-C was 1,800 words long.

A little over half of the first draft was dictated by Baker; this comprised the problem section (which he generally is responsible for when he collaborates) and part of the methods section. Perhaps as part of his intention to speak plainly to the vice-president, Baker wrote the problem section with short, pithy independent clauses that averaged only 11.5 words (compared to 16.4, 17.3, and 15.4 in his first drafts of the problem sections in his other proposals), as shown in Appendix C.9. The greater part of the methods section was dictated by the member of the Firm who had attended the meeting with the client. This second author had longer T-units and independent clauses, though no longer than Baker wrote in other sections, so there was no striking conflict of styles. The second author, however, did write paragraphs with mean lengths considerably longer than those found in Baker's writing: the mean paragraph length in draft 1 was 96, compared to draft 1 means of 48, 51, and 49 in the methods sections that Baker wrote. When the typescripts of these two dictated sections were available, Baker sandwiched the second author's text into the middle of his own. Since the implementation section of this proposal would be quite short, Baker followed his frequent practice of revising draft 1 of the problem and methods sections before writing the nearly *pro forma* final part.

As it turned out, Baker spent the next several days traveling to visit clients, so that the revisions resulting in drafts 2 and 3 were made as time became available during airplane flights, taxicab trips, and other odd moments. Emending in black ink to create draft 2, Baker focused primarily on idea (68 changes) and high affect (20) in the section that he had written. The latter included some subtle but effective rewordings designed to emphasize progress that the vice-president had already made on his own. For example, Baker changed "you will be able" to "you are able," and "improvements which have been made" to "improvements which you have made." Elsewhere, he split in half a passage describing both existing problems and previous improvements made in dealing with those problems, in order to emphasize his recognition of the vice-president's prior efforts. In the methods section, however, the rate of voluntary changes was only 77 (compared to 120 in the problem section); and despite a slightly dominant focus on cohesion (22), Baker reduced the second author's large paragraph mean only from 96 to 88. And because he inserted an idea-oriented sentence group (four structures long), the cohesive ties rate actually declined slightly (from 46 to 41), despite the insertion of three new signal words. Unquestionably the most obvious change in the two parts during this draft, however, was the insertion of one of this unconventional proposal's only three headings ("Customer Service"), along with a recasting of the second author's sole heading (changing "Organizational Productivity Improvement" to "Organizational Effectiveness").

Still unsatisfied, and still on the road, Baker revised the first typescript of the problem and methods sections yet again to create draft 3, this time in blue ink, at voluntary change rates only slightly lower than those in the first revision of the text (92 and 66, compared to 120 and 77 in draft 1). This time, the greatest part of his attention was directed toward idea (35 and 20 in the respective sections) and high affect (23 and 16), with all but a few of the remaining changes involving cohesion and style (about equally divided between goals 6 and 11—that is, between cohesive ties and segmentation of the text for readability). While this now almost illegible typescript was being redone by the word-processing unit, Baker wrote a brief implementation section. Although this passage was not set off with a heading, the familiar topics (along with some of Baker's stock phrases) were clearly distinguishable.

When the typescript of the now complete proposal returned from the word-processing unit, Baker demonstrated his usual reluctance to leave the text alone—for he now revised not only the newly generated implementation section but also the rest of the entire document, from beginning to end. Although the low voluntary change rates for each of the first two sections (42, 32) suggest a desultory going-over, the line of thought in the problem section was considerably altered by the insertion of an eight-structure paragraph that out-lined the client's major concerns and the Firm's general plan of at-tack. Even the few changes to the implementation section proved significant, since among other things Baker removed the nonsensi-cal (and still unexplained) phrase "la bridge" and also raised the cost estimate from $85,000 to $88,000. Since his changes in draft 4 were few but significant, Baker revised another fresh transcript; but most of the changes were minor (for example, "three-phase approach" be-came "three-phased approach"). Even at this stage, however, Baker still was willing to make significant changes, moving a five-structure paragraph (describing what the Firm would discover for the client) so that it followed, rather than preceded, a description of what the Firm *generally* finds in such a study. The effect of this change was to avoid the implication that the Firm had already made up its mind and would just impose canned information and decisions on the vice-president's division; instead, Baker presented himself and the Firm as a knowledgeable group of open-minded consultants ready and willing to lend assistance to this client's "unique" situation. With that accomplished, Baker finally sent the letter to the vice-president.

Proposal Bak-D

Proposal Bak-D demonstrates Baker's important ability to help the client's staff look good while achieving his own purposes—an ability illustrated by the iceberg anecdote in chapter 3, where Baker made a staff person in the client company appear to make a "good suggestion" that Baker had himself presented to the staffer in an ear-lier meeting. A similar instance occurred in the situation surround-ing Bak-D.

Bak-D was written for a large company that produces metal for use by other manufacturers. The company was then considering the feasibility of building a new, $300 million production facility. To de-termine feasibility, it needed to know how much its product would be used by other manufacturers over the next thirty years, what competitors might do during the same time period, what kinds of union activities might be expected, and so on. The proposal would be evaluated and the decision would be made by a fifteen-member committee that Baker thought reflected "a very bureaucratic, bum-bling, traditional organization." Baker never met all the members of the proposal-evaluation committee, but he did know that many of them, the more traditional of the lot, felt their own company could conduct much of the required study of trends themselves. Because of this attitude, and because the company did not often use management consultants, Baker expected to have difficulty persuading them that outside assistance was required—despite the fact that the corporation would base a $300 million investment decision on the study's results, and also despite the fact that a number of careers were on the line.

One of those with a career at stake was the proposal's addressee. In relation to the ranks of the other committee members, he occupied a junior position; but in terms of personal power, he had a forceful personality that the other members would have to reckon with. This person was Baker's main contact at the company, his primary source of information that would help him discover what the company needed and what might influence it to select Baker's Firm instead of another—and therein lies the other example of Baker's savvy use of his potential readers.

Since Baker knew that the situation was highly competitive and that the company was inexperienced in dealing with outside consultants, he also knew that it was important to help his contact look good: if the contact could seem to understand the situation better than the other staffers, and if he were favorably disposed to the Firm, then Baker would have the inside track on producing a winning proposal. So Baker and the contact talked privately about how the company should go about selecting a consulting agency; in particular, they discussed the importance of the company's having a set of criteria to present to potential consultants. In helping his contact develop those criteria, Baker tried to tip the balance in his favor in at least two ways. First, he discussed the convenience and benefits of close contact between consultant and client. It was no accident, of course, that the worldwide headquarters of Baker's firm was located in the same city where the study was to be done. Second, Baker stressed the necessity of hiring a consulting agency that not only had considerable experience in the metals industry (which all the bidding agencies had) but also considerable experience in the automotive industry (which only the Firm had). These two conditions—proximity and automotive experience—became part of the company's criteria for evaluating the consulting agencies. Thus, in helping to develop those criteria, Baker displayed his rare skill: not only to adapt the document to his audience (which he does very well), but also to adapt his audience to the kind of proposal he wants to write.

In its final form, the proposal was, at about 4500 words, the longest of all eight proposals; it committed the Firm to the longest period of work (four months), and it would cost the client the most (about $300,000).

Yet, oddly enough, it was the only proposal for which Baker produced only three drafts (instead of four or five), and it was one of two proposals in which he made only a couple of changes to the implementation section (though, in both instances, that section was revised by another writer). It also presented the most difficulties for analysis of quantifiable features (at least from our approach) because of a composing/revising process that was almost a parody of Baker's usual strategy. In Bak-D, written in about six hours, Baker first dictated what he called a "draft of sections." One of these passages, two typewritten pages long, consisted of the conventional letter opening ("It was a pleasure meeting with you last week to review your thoughts and discuss issues"). Another passsage, a little over one page long, would later constitute the "study strategy" part of the problem section. Next came a fourteen-page passage, the first eleven pages of which would constitute most of the methods section, and the last three pages of which would comprise part of the problem section. At several points in this fourteen-page stretch, Baker dictated notes not to his typist but to himself, as in the following:

> Note on Step 3. Be sure to include econometric forecast / George Mason. Also involve him in the secondary Firm specialist step and the words that would go with that: George Mason, econometric forecaster, who accurately forecasted within 4% the valley and rebound of sales in North America at a time when industry and company sources, as well as associations were forecasting a leveling.

In other words, while there was no question that Baker approached this text with the familiar generic script for a proposal in mind, he seems to have had less of an idea what specific line of thought his proposal would take or how the available data would support such an arrangement. Essentially, he wrote out three "arguments" and then recast them into an overriding line of thought. In so doing, he made the most dramatic changes in a text made by either author.

Once Baker had a typescript of what he had dictated (which we are calling draft 1, since the various segments had most of the characteristics of the problem and methods sections), he set about a very extensive cut-and-paste rearrangement, accompanied by handwritten revisions in blue ink. As a result, draft 2 had very high rates for all six processes, but particularly high rates for insertions and moves (see Appendix C.10). For revisions that involved more than a single structure, eleven moves were comprised, respectively, of 10, 2, 2, 4, 2, 25, 2, 6, 17, 17, and 3 structures—a very great amount of reorganizing compared to his normal practice. His unusual cut-and-paste activity distorted all of the rates for draft 2 in both the problem and methods sections, since, as noted earlier, we determine rates by dividing the number of changes by the number of T-units in the draft being revised (and then multiplying by 100).

This distortion occurred because of two factors in our method. First, we determine revision rates by dividing the number of changes to a draft by the number of T-units in the text (or a part of the text) before this set of changes was made. For example, the first part of draft 1 might have 250 T-units. In creating draft 2, the writer might make 50 changes (insertions and deletions) to this part. In such a case, the rate of revisions would be 50 divided by 250 (yielding 0.2) times 100 (yielding 20). A problem would occur if one of the 50 changes was a move of a long passage from another part of the text into this part. Suppose that this move imported 100 T-units from the other section and that 24 of the 50 changes made in this revising session were made in the 100 imported T-units. Under these circumstances, there would be several ways of computing the rate. First, one could count the move and the 24 changes made in the imported passage as one move. Thus, the rate would be 26 divided by 250, for a rate of 10 per 100 T-units. Second, one could treat the number of imported T-units as part of the original text; that is, one could add the 100 imported T-units to the original 250. Then one would add the number of changes made to both the original text and the imported passage (24 plus 1 plus 25, yielding 50). After that, one would compute the rate: 50 divided by 350, yielding a rate of 14. Third, as just noted, one could divide the total number of changes to both the original and the imported T-units by the number of T-units in the original (50 divided by 250), yielding a rate of 20 per 100 T-units. Of course, such distortions do not occur if rates are figured for the whole text, since in that case moves do not affect the number of

T-units. But if we focus on rates for whole texts, then another sort of distortion occurs, because our study shows that writers revise different sections in different ways and at different rates.

To be as consistent as possible, we selected the third alternative, figuring rates by dividing the number of changes by the number of original T-units. For this reason, the rate for the problem section (into which much material was moved) is distorted high, and the rate for the methods section (from which much material was moved) is distorted low in draft 2 of Bak-D. Even so, the proportions between rates continue to be indicative of Baker's concerns in each section. (To gain a rough idea of the rate of revising activity expended on material first generated—regardless of where it ended up after any moves—one may halve the rates listed for the problem section and double those listed for the methods section.)

In his draft 2 changes to the problem section, Baker focused on idea and high-affect changes (56 percent of the total number of revisions), the most dramatic of which involved the moves that resulted in a substantially new line of thought. But he also devoted a good deal of attention to cohesion, style, and usage, so that the number of headings per T-unit climbed from 3 to 4 and the paragraph mean declined from 97 to 74—both of these trends reflecting Baker's concern to segment the text for readability. The rate of usage errors also declined, but the percent of weak clauses rose, since many of the imported T-units were of the clausal-frame type ("The client believes that . . .") that often supplies a necessary distinction for the rhetorical situation. That is, a proposal is judged not merely by whether it makes true statements about a company's problems, but also by whether it makes accurate statements about what the company believes its problems to be. This was particularly necessary in Bak-D, where Baker needed to shape the responses of readers unfamiliar with (and in some cases antagonistic to) Baker's plans for helping them solve their problem.

In his draft 2 revisions to the methods section, Baker remained highly interested in idea and high affect (over 42 percent of his changes), but he focused mainly on cohesion, making changes directed toward every goal in that orientation. As a result, rates for ties and headings increased, although the paragraph, T-unit, and independent clause means stayed relatively even.

While draft 2 was off to the word-processing unit, the implementation section was generated and included in the resulting typescript of draft 3. For this draft, Baker's voluntary change rate was reduced to a desultory 31 in the problem section and 36 in the methods section. In both parts, he devoted over half of his attention to idea and high affect, with the rest given to cohesion and style. He ignored usage entirely. The implementation section received a number of revisions by another member of the Firm's proposal planning team; and while three marks by Baker indicate that he reviewed those changes, he left the text almost exactly as he found it.

Franklin's Proposals: Overview

Franklin's writing process differs from Baker's both in technique and in extent. The key difference is that Franklin does not dictate his first drafts, but rather generates them in pencil; as a result, his second drafts consist not of revisions to a typescript of dictation, but rather of penciled revisions to a draft written by hand on lined paper. Although his usual practice is to make replacements by erasing and then by writing over the erasure, he agreed (for our study) to cross out the text to be replaced. Nevertheless, some of his first drafts did contain erasures, and thus part of his revising process was lost from our observation. However, when we inspected the handwritten drafts closely to estimate how much of the text had been erased, we found that less than a single line per page of handwritten text had been erased and then written over; as a result, we believe that very little of Franklin's written material was not recovered by our method of analysis.

In another procedural matter, we assumed that Franklin's penciled revisions to his handwritten originals correspond to Baker's handwritten revisions to the typescript of his dictated originals; as a result, we have treated such penciled revisions as constituting draft 2 of his proposals. Such an assumption, of course, needs to be tested by subsequent research.

Proposals Fra-A and Fra-B

Proposals Fra-A and Fra-B were both addressed to the same reader (call him Smith), the general manager of a large manufacturing division of a major American corporation. The Firm had previously done two or three studies for Smith, but the most recent one had occurred three to five years earlier. Franklin did not believe the corporation had hired any other consulting agencies in the meantime, since one of Smith's key staff members told Franklin that "Smith isn't going to make a move without your firm being involved." Thus, Franklin (who had consulted for Smith before) had established credibility going in, so much so that both situations were probably noncompetitive. As Franklin points out, however, a lack of competition does not necessarily mean the proposals are assured of winning, because if clients are dissatisfied with the proposal, they can always decide to look elsewhere or to do the study themselves.

Fra-A proposed to examine the feasibility of relocating Smith's division to a new geographic area. In his preproposal meeting with Smith, Franklin determined four key issues that he later addressed as the following questions in the proposal's "objectives" section:

> What steps are required to execute the relocation?
> What will be the cost of relocation?
> To what extent can manufacturing resource requirements (space, equipment, manpower) be reduced through a move?
> What operating benefits would result from a move?

The task would require six weeks of consulting at a total cost of about $55,000 (plus expenses). In its final version, the proposal was 1,443 words long.

Once the feasibility study was concluded, the division had authorization to pursue the idea further and asked the Firm for a proposal (Fra-B) on plant location. In the report presentation for the first study, however, Franklin had some problems with a junior colleague who fouled up the presentation in some significant ways. Because of that problem, Franklin was concerned that the situation for the second study would be competitive, but this turned out not to be the case, undoubtedly because of the Firm's successful record with Smith's company.

In particular, proposal Fra-B involved finding a site for an additional manufacturing facility to produce a new part that was vital for military and commercial aircraft. The new part was technologically superior, the corporation felt, to others on the market, and thus they anticipated a great increase in production volume, necessitating additional capacity. Another facility was also necessary because of the quickness with which the part had to be delivered: if an airliner in Germany were grounded because it needed the part, the corporation would have to deliver on time or lose the customer. Moreover, because the company's current production facility existed in a highly unionized environment and was thus subject to strikes, the corporation needed another location to assure timely delivery of its product. But the potential union problems were only one factor: a tornado or a fire would also inhibit production if the product were manufactured at only one facility.

According to Franklin, proposal Fra-B (like Fra-A) was pretty "matter of fact," since "we not only had done work for the company before, but we had done the same type of work for them." Moreover, Franklin was advised by Smith to use the same approach the Firm had employed in a previous study for him. Thus, one whole set of rhetorical decisions was already made for Franklin, and so was another. Smith was definitely the key decision maker, so much so that he never even showed the first proposal to his staff. The study proposed in Fra-B required two phases of five and six weeks, respectively, at a cost of $60,000. In its final version, the proposal was 1,574 words long.

Before we begin to analyze Franklin's composing and revising strategies and their effects on Fra-A, Fra-B, and the other two proposals, we should recall the general differences between his prose style and Baker's (as discussed earlier in this chapter). We should also note that, since his proposals are shorter, the number of T-units in a given section may be quite small. As a result, the rates and percentages are much more volatile in Franklin's proposals than in Baker's, since fewer changes have greater effects. In particular, rates can give an impression of much greater activity than actually occurred. For example, the problem section of Fra-A had only 15 T-units. In revising this section to create draft 2, Franklin made only 17 voluntary changes, for a rate of 114. (Voluntary rates shown on the charts are sums of the five orientation rates; due to rounding, they sometimes vary slightly from a true rate of voluntary changes divided by number of T-units.) Of these changes, 12 were oriented toward idea, three toward cohesion, and one each toward style and usage. Thus, even though he made only one style change, the style rate was 7; and since 7 can sound like a lot more than 1, we need to be careful not to overestimate the amount of activity implied by the rates, at least in the short implementation sections and in some of the relatively short problem sections. Similarly, even though the net effect of Franklin's insertions, deletions, and replacements in draft 2 of the problem section was to increase the number of words in the section by only 19, the section's T-unit mean rose somewhat sharply (from 18.5 to 19.7).

Thus, relatively small changes in short sections can have relatively large effects on measures of quantitative elements in the text. Even so, the effects of the changes on the text itself are no less real, even if the statistics exaggerate their impact a little. For example, if a long T-unit were inserted into a passage, the T-unit mean would be altered more if the original passage had been five T-units long than if it had been twenty T-units long; and while we must keep this statistical exaggeration in mind, we should not lose sight of the fact that a long T-unit inserted into a five-T-unit passage would have a very striking effect on the text. With these considerations in mind, we can turn to an analysis of Franklin's strategy in revising Fra-A and Fra-B, starting with the first of these.

After the initial meeting with the client, Franklin wrote out the problem and methods section of draft 1, writing in pencil on lined paper. He then revised these sections (also in pencil), creating draft 2. While the typescript was being prepared, he wrote the implementation section in pencil, and also revised it in pencil. As noted earlier, according to our approach, all of the material *generated* in pencil (in the problem, methods, and implementation sections) constitutes draft 1. The revisions to all three parts constitute draft 2.

As Appendix C.11 shows, in draft 2 of Fra-A, Franklin's moderate voluntary change rate (114) oriented largely toward idea (80), involved only minor insertions, deletions, or replacements of a word or phrase (for example, "basic" to "major," "operations" to "divisions"). The voluntary change rate was higher in the methods section (143) because of increased activity oriented toward high affect and style. The high-affect changes were directed toward several goals. To avoid an insult, Franklin changed from saying that the Firm would "carry out its own analysis" of data supplied by Smith (which sounds distrustful) to saying that the Firm would "make an assessment" (which sounds thorough). To build credit, he changed the distant-sounding "the study team" to the more personal "we"; and instead of saying that the Firm would take steps to "minimize the effort" of conducting the study (which sounds lazy), he said the

Firm would "minimize the time" (which sounds efficient). To feed a wish, he emphasized the positive by changing "tasks that will be involved in relocating" to "tasks required to effectively relocate," and he also changed the hypothetical "would" and "plan to" to "will" (for example, "We plan to do this" to "We will do this"). This pattern of greater voluntary activity in the methods section than in the problem section is typical of Franklin's approach, occurring in nearly every draft of every part and holding true for the total number of each part's revisions in all but one proposal (Fra-C). In this respect, Franklin's approach to the functional parts of a proposal differs significantly from Baker's, since Baker always revises the problem section at a greater voluntary rate than he does the methods section.

In the implementation section of draft 2 of Fra-A, Franklin demonstrated both writers' typically increased amount of attention to high affect in those sections, since an implementation section's function is to describe the Firm's staff and to bond with the client by means of a "complimentary close" to the letter-format proposal. As it turned out, these were the last revisions Franklin made to the implementation section of Fra-A (except for a single idea change in draft 4). There could be no clearer evidence of his lack of interest in tinkering with the text—that is, in giving it the sophisticated polish that Baker characteristically seeks.

When Franklin received the typescript of draft 2 of the first two sections, he went over it twice—once in black ink (draft 3), then again in blue ink (draft 4). Neither set of changes had much effect on the measures of the quantitative elements of style. In draft 3, both sections received some attention to cohesion, but Franklin was merely changing major headings to minor ones—changes that were perhaps more akin to correcting typographical errors than to arranging or rearranging the text. And while T-unit and independent clause length declined slightly in both sections in the final draft, the decrease was due to the insertion of new, short sentences oriented toward idea or high affect—for example, sentences about the speed with which the Firm could complete its study.

All things considered, Franklin's approach to Fra-A is emblematic of his general concept of composing and revising: he knows what line of thought he will take, he writes it down, he knocks some of the rough places off, and he sends the proposal to the client. But while his strategy of revising Fra-A serves as a useful emblem, it should not be considered a stereotype. To enforce this point, we need only examine his process of writing Fra-B, which, as noted earlier, was a highly similar proposal written to the same client as Fra-B, and which was composed only two months later. Franklin generated the first draft of this proposal in two sessions. In the first, he wrote out the problem section in ink; in the second, he wrote out the methods and implementation sections in pencil, boilerplating freely from a previous site-selection proposal written for another client. Generally speaking, the quantifiable features of this draft (shown in Appendix C.12) do not vary much from the usual rates and percentages, except that the T-unit means for the problem and methods sections were in effect reversed: that of the problem section was quite high for that section (26.2), while that of the methods section was somewhat low (20.9). The high mean in the problem section was caused by a high percentage of weak clauses, brought about because Franklin recapitulated the general manager's remarks from their earlier meetings:

> The client believes that the new technology inherent in the manufacture of its product will lead to a dramatic increase in demand for that product. It believes, too, that its development program and military aircraft experience give it a competitive edge that will enable it to capture a significant share of the available market.

The low mean in the methods section, however, appears to have occurred by chance.

Franklin produced draft 2 in his usual manner, making changes in pencil—except for the boilerplated passages. These, which had literally been cut from the typescript of another proposal and pasted onto the lined paper on which Franklin characteristically writes, were revised in red ink. As he went over the problem and methods sections, Franklin departed from his stereotypic process in two major respects. First, he revised at a higher rate than usual (182). Second, he paid more than his usual amount of attention to cohesion and style. In particular, all but one of his style changes in these two sections had the goal of conciseness. This extraordinary attention brought the T-unit and independent clause means down in the problem section, but failed to do so in the methods section because of a relatively high rate of idea changes (56), many of them insertions or replacements that increased the size of the text. Third, and perhaps most remarkably, Franklin made a very great number of changes whose effect was to make the concepts in the proposal more specific.

Some of this can be explained by the influence of situational norms operating on the boilerplated material. For example, the boilerplate listed the following "factor" as one to be covered by the study: "Energy resources and availability." The new client, however, needed a particular type of energy for its manufacturing process, so Franklin revised the phrase to "Availability of natural gas." Similarly, he changed the boilerplate's general phrase "your operation" to the client-specific phrase "your proposed operation."

For many other passages in the boilerplated material, however, there was no pressing need for a change, since the boilerplate, while somewhat general and vague, was no less relevant to the new client than to the old. Even so, Franklin revised many of these. Here, again, different motives appear to have been at work. In some of the changes, Franklin moved from writer-based to reader-based prose. For example, thinking of the task that he would need to perform in this study, Franklin first wrote that a touchstone or standard-setting community would be "selected" by the Firm. In draft 2, he considered the idea from the client's perspective, and wrote that the ideal community would be "identified" by the Firm; the implication now was that the Firm would "identify" while the client would "select." Elsewhere, Franklin first wrote that such touchstone communities "are" identified for a particular purpose; in revising, he adopted the reader's perspective, and wrote that such communities "will be" identified (that is, for this particular purpose *for this particular client*).

Other changes made to the text were neither required by the new client's situation nor prompted by the need to adopt the client's perspective; they simply made the information clearer. For example, in draft 1 Franklin said the Firm would verify information about the touchstone communities by contacting "knowledgeable sources in the area"; in draft 2, he said they would contact "knowledgeable sources in each of the areas being analyzed." In draft 1, he referred to a "recommendation" to be made by the Firm; in draft 2, he changed that to the more specific "recommended location." In draft 1, he wrote "geographic area"; in draft 2, he changed that to "operating environment." This desire for specificity and accuracy is typical of Franklin. In fact, in another proposal, he changed the boilerplated phrase "over 75 years" to "over 78 years"—not because the number 78 was more meaningful or impressive to the client, and certainly not because it mattered to anyone else whether the time-span had been 75 or 78 years, but simply because it was more accurate. This habit of mind may account for part of Franklin's success as a management consultant, as well as for his success as a proposal writer.

In the implementation section, his changes in draft 2 focused on idea and high affect; but he also paid a good deal of attention to style (conciseness), so that the independent clause mean declined sharply (from 21.5 to 18.3), as did the T-unit mean (from 23.5 to 20.2).

When the typescript of draft 2 was returned to him, Franklin revised it in red ink. In the first two sections, he focused mainly on idea and high affect, continuing to make client-specific changes of the sort just described. On the whole, though, these somewhat desultory changes had no significant effect on the quantifiable descriptors.

Proposal Fra-C

Proposal Fra-C was written for a company quite different from the one addressed in Fra-A and Fra-B—a much smaller, relatively unsophisticated company that knew little about the matters the firm would be proposing. In Fra-A and Fra-B, Franklin assumed that, when he "made a statement, they knew what I was talking about"; but in proposal Fra-C, he "felt that I had to walk them through rather specifically, and very clearly tell them what it was that we were going to do." Whereas the Fra-A/Fra-B manufacturer was "technologically oriented" and composed of "hard hitters, the heavy hitters coming out of automotive and aerospace," those at company Fra-C were friendly and "humanistic," and were not at all sure what kind of study they wanted. At that time, they were trying to develop a strategy for increased growth and profitability during an expected economic upturn. Basically, their problem was that they were not sure how much growth (if any) the company's manufacturing division could sustain. Thus, they were exploring the possibility of having the Firm "audit" various aspects of that division.

When Franklin made his initial visit, about three months before he was asked to write the proposal, he went with two other specialists to talk about several specific areas that might be examined.

At first, the company appeared to favor a limited investigation of just one area, but made no commitment to authorize it. Months later, after Franklin made repeated phone calls, the company decided on a full study of all the areas discussed at the first meeting.

The company's reluctance to decide on the study's scope stemmed not only from their inexperience, but also from a volatile political situation in the division to be audited. Several of the company's leaders felt that the division had problems; for example, the vice-president of finance told Franklin he just was not getting from manufacturing what was needed to run the company. But the vice-president of manufacturing was the son of the company's former chairman, and he carried a lot of weight in strategy decisions. Thus, even after delivering the proposal, Franklin did not get the go-ahead for yet another month because the company's chairman had to clear everything with the vice-president of manufacturing.

Nevertheless, in writing the proposal to the chairman, Franklin felt no need to avoid the sensitive issues. Since so much was wrong at the company, and since so many of the principal players knew there was so much wrong, Franklin felt justified in sidestepping the former chairman's son: "I was not trying to write behind the scenes for the vice-president of manufacturing; I was writing to the chairman because, after all, he is the major stockholder in the company and it's his responsibility to run the company well. And if manufacturing isn't being run well, the company is not going to run well." The project would require five weeks of consulting time, at a cost of about $60,000 (plus expenses). In its final version, the proposal was 1,337 words long.

Overall, Franklin's writing of this proposal was quite similar to that for proposal Fra-A. He first generated the problem and methods sections and the staffing and deliverables passages of the implementation section, and then he revised them (all in pencil), creating drafts 1 and 2 of those sections. While a typescript of draft 2 was being prepared, he generated and revised the timing, costs, and qualifications segments of the implementation section (using three long pieces of boilerplate). These passages received no further revision after the penciled changes to the original draft, and went to the client "as is." Thus, data in Appendix C.13 about the implementation section of draft 3 are somewhat misleading, since only about one-fourth of the section was actually revised.

Like his overall revising procedures, Franklin's focus in respect to the orientations and goals in Fra-C was quite similar to that of Fra-A, as shown in Appendix C.13. The most striking difference between the last drafts of the two proposals is his much greater use of cohesive ties in Fra-C's problem and methods sections (41 vs. 18, and 81 vs. 26, respectively). Clearly, his desire to lead his inexperienced, unfocused audience through his line of thought had a marked impact on the text—not only in the increased incidence of cohesive ties, but also in the accompanying increase in T-unit means.

Proposal Fra-D

Proposal Fra-D, written during an economic recession, presented the Firm's plan for a relocation study for a division of a Fortune 500 company. Initially, it presented Franklin with two difficulties. First, according to Franklin, the division was a "chintzy outfit and not forward-thinking in terms of investing." That is, the client saw no need for full-scale feasibility and site-location studies, so the plan had to be "confined to what we consider the first phase of a comprehensive manufacturing facility relocation study." Second, a rather large number of consulting firms were offering competitive bids in response to the request for proposals. Normally, Franklin and his firm would not even have pursued the project, but business had been bad during the recession and Franklin had not done a study for months.

The proposal's final draft quoted fees of $25,000, even though Franklin's firm had originally proposed a study for about $10,000 more, based on its estimate of the time and effort needed to solve the client's problems. When Franklin discussed the larger study scope and fees with the client, however, the latter was shocked by the price: other firms, the client said, had come in at around $15,000. But those firms, advised Franklin, did not have the resources to do the kind of study needed. As a compromise, Franklin pared down the study's scope and price. The text that Franklin sent to the client took the form of a two-page, single-spaced letter to the company's manager (the only person he had contacted at the company), along with an eight-page segment constituting the proposal proper.

Two features of this proposal are particularly noteworthy. First, because of the client's reluctance, Franklin took special care to explain the client's problem in detail—both to illustrate the Firm's understanding of the client's situation and to convince the client that its problems were severe enough to require an unexpectedly high expenditure for consultants. As a result, the problem section of Fra-D constituted nearly 60 percent of the entire proposal—a far greater percentage than in any of his other three proposals (20, 18, and 26 percent, respectively), as shown in Appendix C.14. And when Franklin revised this section to create draft 2, his rate of high-affect revisions (28, accompanied by an idea change rate of 85) was atypically high for that section.

The second noteworthy factor about the revisions in Fra-D was that another member of the firm—a less experienced and less skilled writer than Franklin—had generated the first draft of the methods section. As a result, when Franklin revised to create draft 2 of this section, his cohesion, style, and usage rates were extraordinarily high, since he needed to make many changes in order to blend the second writer's passages in with his own. For example, Franklin had to recast the second author's frequent minor-form independent clauses ("Meet with you and other personnel") to major-form clauses like those he used in the problem section ("We will meet with you and other personnel").

In this chapter, we have examined in detail the differences between the cultural and personal norms that motivate Baker and Franklin, and we have seen that differences in their respective styles of prose are matched by differences in their strategies for generating and revising a text. We have also noted in detail the ways in which both product and process are affected by audience and by other factors governing the rhetoric of a proposal in a business setting. In the final section of this study, we will review the main findings of chapters 3 and 4 and then briefly discuss some implications of our method and results for scholars and teachers.

Conclusion

WHAT, THEN, MAY WE CONCLUDE FROM OUR STUDY OF THIS FIRM
and the eight proposals by Baker and Franklin? In answering this
question, we will first summarize what we have reported in chapters 3 and 4. Then we will suggest how our findings are relevant to
theoretical and pedagogical issues in rhetoric and composition.

Summary of Findings

From the perspective of what might be called the "macroprocess"
of composing, both writers demonstrate clear stages of prewriting
(described mainly in chapter 3) and of generating and revising the
text (described mainly in chapter 4). Baker organizes his notes, dic-
tates at least a major section (with no doubling back for revision, because of the very nature of dictation), and then revises each typescript, with very few of his changes involving insertions, deletions,
or moves of material larger than a word or phrase. Franklin's macroprocess is even more linear: he thinks, he writes in longhand, he
revises a typescript, and he sends the proposal off—and even fewer
of his changes involve units larger than a word or phrase.

To some extent, the "staged" aspects of their composing processes
are somewhat obscured by the fact that they generate and revise in
rhythmic waves. Baker typically alternates text-generating sessions
with text-revising sessions—not, however, because he is reviewing
and evaluating the text in order to see where he might go next (that

is, how he might recast the line of thought or redefine the overall purpose of his text), but simply because he is usually pressed for time. As a result, he generates one part and, while it is being typed up, generates another; and when the second segment is being typed up, he revises the first segment and/or generates a third. In Franklin's case, the opportunity for recursive rather than staged composing is much greater, since, by writing in longhand, he can revise as he goes along, revise when he has finished a segment, revise when he has finished a draft, or revise at all of these moments. And while, as we noted earlier, our approach does not allow us to observe what went on while Franklin was generating the first draft of a text, we do know that he made very few erasures in writing Fra-A (written before he agreed not to erase but rather to cross out and write over) and that he made few "false starts" in the other three proposals (that is, few passages which were aborted in favor of another). Thus, there is little evidence of revision occurring *while* he generated the first draft, rather than *afterward*. This evidence supports Franklin's claim that he revises little as he writes, making most of his changes in a final reading of the whole text or section. So in Franklin's case, too, the writer did not review or edit his work much as his ideas were committed to the page, but rather revised in stages quite distinct from the episodes of generating text.

For both writers, therefore, we found no evidence that their rhythmic alternations of generating and revising texts were truly recursive, in that the revision of (say) the problem section before the generation of the methods section had no impact upon the methods section. That is, the writers did not go back to revise one section in preparation for writing a subsequent one; in Flower and Hayes' terms, the revision of one section did not alter the overall plan or the goals for the subsequent section. Rather, the alternation of generating and revising was almost always imposed by a tight timetable for producing the proposal; if the writers had had time to produce a whole text at one sitting, they very well might have, and subsequently could have revised the whole text in one sitting.

As we have seen in chapters 3 and 4, a number of aspects of the writing environment influence this macroprocess. In particular, they influence the limitation of the writers' revisions to relatively small elements of the text. First, their writing is a task-specific response assigned by the Firm (rather than self-initiated); so they do not "grow" into a sense of purpose, but begin with it. Second, their proposals always develop the same overall line of thought (problem, methods, implementation); so they need not search for or develop an appropriate organization for their ideas. Third, their highly conventional line of thought is applied to a fairly limited range of subjects (manufacturing and marketing trends for Baker, and relocation feasibility and site selection for Franklin); so they do not need to familiarize themselves with a new area of inquiry. Fourth, many of their strategies in bidding for jobs and their procedures for producing proposals are prescribed by the Firm; so they do not need to develop new arguments or approaches. Fifth, they both use the Firm's word-processing unit; so fresh typescripts are readily available. Sixth, deadlines for producing finished proposals are normally quite short; so they are forced to adopt relatively time-efficient methods and to prioritize goals.

From the perspective of what might be called the "microprocess" of revising, both writers' dynamic patterns of revisions from draft to draft exhibit the multiplicity and simultaneity of rhetorical and linguistic concerns associated with recursiveness. In all drafts, their changes are oriented as much toward ideas and high affect as toward cohesion, style, and usage—that is, toward modifications of the information, ideas, or argument of the document, as much as toward what might be called "text polishing," "cleaning up," or "repairing mechanics." Later drafts do not ignore ideas to focus on (say) usage, but rather maintain a pattern of multiple focus on all aspects of the document. In Baker's case, however, and particularly in the problem section of Bak-A, there appear to be rhythmic waves of attention—a revising session mainly focusing on altering ideas and signaling connections, followed by a session mainly focusing on cleaning up language (especially for conciseness), followed by a session primarily of renewed attention to ideas, followed by a final session of polishing text and making very minor adjustments to the sense.

And just as macroprocesses are altered by factors beyond the writers' control, so too are microprocesses. In analyzing draft-by-draft patterns of revision, we found great variability in rates and proportions of attention to the various orientations—in proposals on the same subject to different readers, and even in similar proposals written to the same reader. A number of factors about the writers' situation underlie this variability: the degree of familiarity with the reader or readers; the number of readers; the knowledge and attitudes of the readers (especially when there is more than one reader or decision maker); the writers' or the Firm's preexisting reputation or credibility; the difficulty of the task, whether figured in terms of typicality, scope, or abstractness; the presence or absence of a second writer; the use of boilerplate; the importance of the task (in terms of the Firm's interest in making money); the quality of one's typist or word processor (as in abundance or sparseness of typographic errors); and the demands of superiors or colleagues in reviewing the text.

Affecting all of these is the amount of time available to produce the document. Such availability can affect macroprocess, for example, in that some "immediate-need" texts (such as memos) may be planned only briefly and generated hurriedly, with virtually no revising of the first draft. And time constraints can affect microprocess in that they may influence the writer's very notion of a "draft"; that is, they may partly determine the point at which the writer treats the existing text as a temporary or final product. This issue of what constitutes a draft is sidestepped by studies using artificial composing environments, where subjects generate discourse in one session and revise it during another, with the output from each session considered a draft. But in a nonartificial situation, what the researchers and the subjects consider a draft might be markedly different. For example, in self-sponsored writing under ideal conditions, a writer might compose and revise for a certain period of time, until something tells him or her that enough time has been spent on that stretch of discourse and that more will be gained by setting the text aside than by continuing to work it over. In such a case, a draft is the product of an at least partly conscious decision. Even under such ideal conditions, of course, space may become a factor even though time is not; that is, a writer might wish to continue revising, but the composing surface (the literal sheet on which the text is recorded) might be so littered with emendations that it must be abandoned and the output called a draft.

But under the working conditions of a business environment, constraints of both time and space might significantly influence the writing process. For example, if the writer were a management consultant for the Firm, composing at the office, a conscious decision or lack of space still might lead him or her to leave off generating or revising in order to have a fresh typescript prepared. But if the writer were away from the office for a week, scribbling down parts of the proposal in airplanes and airport limos and taxicabs, so that time constraints were imposed by the duration of a flight or a car ride, then the drafts and composing strategies might be considerably different. For instance, Baker's proposal Bak-C was revised over several days while he traveled from client to client. Leaving on the trip with a typescript of draft 1 in hand, Baker revised it in bits and pieces, first going through the text (sporadically) in one color of ink, then having a false-start session (in pencil) during which only a couple of changes were made (treated as a "run-through" and thus included as data for draft 3), and then going over the typescript again in another color of ink—again doing so as time allowed over a period of days. As a result, the original draft 1 typescript was so nearly illegible that, when a new typescript incorporating both sets of revisions was available, Baker revised it and then had another typescript (draft 4) prepared for a final set of revisions (draft 5). Had he written the proposal entirely in his office, his revising process might have been different.

Yet another factor influences both macro- and microprocesses of revision: the predominant mode (for example, argument, exposition, narration) of the text or the part of the text being revised. Mode affects not only the product (as measured by words per T-unit, and so forth) but also the amount, the nature, and perhaps the quality of revisions made. We found consistent differences in each writer's strategies of revision for the problem, methods, and implementation sections, respectively. Just as sentence-combining research has had to take mode into account in developing pedagogy, in designing empirical studies, and in assessing results of studies, so too must studies of the revising process. For, as our study clearly indicates, process and product are interdependent: the composing and revising process results in a document, but the nature or function of the desired product affects the process used to create it.

A final dominant factor that our study found to affect revision involves the writer's verbal skills and characteristic configurations of linguistic and rhetorical features—in a word, the writer's style, whether of the product or of the composing process. As we have seen, Baker is a tinkerer: he has a wider repertoire of linguistic and rhetorical devices, and he spends more time fashioning the text after the basic line of thought and level of development have been laid down. Franklin, however skilled he may be in comparison with other groups of writers (for example, college students or college teachers and researchers in his field), has a different approach, relying more heavily on graphic devices to supplement the limitations of his linguistic repertoire. Partly as a result of these language-oriented constraints, he revises at a lesser rate, though he does revise effectively and adequately for his task and readers.

Implications for Research and Pedagogy

Our study appears to contribute both to the methodology and to the substance of current research in rhetoric and composition. So far as method is concerned, of course, we have discovered several constraints on our approach to the study of revision. The most obvious is that it is extremely time-consuming. Any future study using this approach should take advantage of more advanced computer techniques for recording, coding, and analyzing texts. Interviews with writers should be more structured, so that more information can be accumulated earlier to guide coding and subsequent analysis of texts. At the same time, single texts should be coded by several researchers working independently, so that the coding (and hence the analysis) can depend less on decision by consensus and more on decision by quantifiable measures. Finally, a greater number of texts and writers should be analyzed, so that statistical tests of reliability may be applied to the apparent similarities and differences.

Despite these constraints, however, the approach we have presented appears to provide useful information about the revising process as it occurs in one actual business environment. With appropriate modifications of the coding procedure used in this study, the seven variables of composition might serve as a useful point of departure for studies involving larger numbers of writers, writers in different environments (for example, the research laboratory, the government agency, the freshman composition classroom), and writers of different kinds of documents (for example, familiar essays, research reports, business letters).

Since we have observed highly staged writing processes in the proposals written by Baker and Franklin, our study's method and results would appear to conflict with recursive models of the composing process, particularly as described by Nancy Sommers in her important essay "Revision Strategies of Student Writers and Experienced Adult Writers" (1980). In that essay, which was so useful in bringing to light the importance of recursiveness in writing, Sommers made several claims which sharpened her argument at the time but which may now need to be refined. First, in contrasting "linear" and "recursive" models of the writing process, Sommers claimed that in a linear model "each stage . . . must be exclusive (distinct from the other stages) or else it becomes trivial and counterproductive to refer to these junctures as 'stages'" (379). This claim is not explained or justified, despite the fact that it runs counter to accepted practice in many areas of scientific and scholarly inquiry. Very often, a linear model is used to conceptualize a process in which each stage is not absolutely distinct from any other stage or in which the boundaries between stages are not clear. To take a familiar example from the sciences, the process of mitosis is not rigidly segmented or episodic, but occurs in one steady movement; the fluidity of this change, however, does not eliminate the utility of conceiving of the process in terms of stages (prophase, metaphase, anaphase, telophase). In language study, too, the usefulness of conceptualized stages is common. For example, Albert C. Baugh (1957) prefaces his overview of the periods in the history of English by noting the difference between the process itself and the concept which allows us to understand the main stages in the process: "The evolution of English in the fifteen hundred years of its existence in England has been an unbroken one. Within this development, however, it is possible to recognize three main periods. Like all divisions in history the periods of the English language are matters of convenience and the dividing lines between them purely arbitrary. There is no break in the process of continuous transition. But within each of the periods it is possible to recognize certain broad characteristics and certain special developments that take place" (59). Thus, if one wishes to claim that, broadly speaking, many writers' composing processes may be conceived as occurring in three stages, and if this concept is pedagogically useful, then the idea of linearity in the overall act of composing (that is, the macroprocess) is not inherently trivial.

On the contrary, as writing teachers have long known (less as theory than as a working notion), rigidly imposed staging of the composing process can be pedagogically useful. In regard to invention (or "planning" or "prewriting"), for example, it is sometimes useful to brainstorm—that is, solely to generate and write down all ideas that occur, without reviewing, evaluating, or organizing them. In regard to generating ("translating," "writing") a text, too, it is frequently useful to urge unskilled writers not to be recursive: "Don't worry about spelling or usage in this draft; just try to get your ideas down on paper, without stopping and going back to change something you think might be grammatically incorrect." In this example, of course, revising ("stopping and going back") is equivalent to editing for usage, but it need not be; many teachers find it useful to tell some students, "Don't worry about details in this draft; just try to sketch out your main line of thought. You can fill in the details later." Finally, in regard to revising, it can be useful for learners to stage the process: "Read through your essay the first time for ideas; then read through it again looking for problems in cohesion; then look through it once more for problems in style or usage." Indeed, such staging in some nonacademic settings is highly conscious, as described by Mary Fran Beuhler in "Controlled Flexibility in Technical Editing: The Levels-of-Edit Concept at JPL" (1977).

A second troublesome claim made by Sommers is that "by staging revision after enunciation, the linear models reduce revision in writing, as in speech, to no more than an afterthought. In this way such models make the study of revision impossible" (379). The first part of this remark quite unnecessarily reduces any "second thought" to the pejorative category of "afterthought." But everyday experience is replete with instances of second thoughts being just as important, if not more important, than first thoughts. For example, we might see something on sale and decide to buy it, paying with a check; but even as we write out the check, we suddenly remember that our paycheck will not be deposited in the bank until the next day; so we decide to use a credit card, or postpone our purchase, or go without. Similarly, in a rhetorical situation, a male chauvinist college president writing a memo to his administrative staff might first generate the sentence "Each administrator may bring his wife to the dinner." Later, however, as he reads through the typescript of his dictated memo, he might as an "after" or "second" thought remember that the college has recently hired a female assistant vice-president for student affairs (in response to an affirmative action program imposed by a Federal court). Thus, whether from raised consciousness or from fear of antagonizing a court-appointed mediator, he might change the sentence to "Administrators may bring their spouses to the dinner." We might well lament the fact that this change occurred to the college president only as an afterthought; but from a rhetorical perspective, the change would be an important "second thought," or "revision," or "re-seeing of what he had said originally." In other words, even if revisions consist only of minor adjustments of the text (in terms of its size, informational content, or overall line of thought), such adjustments might yet be rhetorically significant—particularly if they focus on tone or other reader-oriented aspects of the document being composed. Sommers' further assertion—that a model based on stages and "afterthoughts" makes the study of revision impossible—is simply inexplicable from the point of view of our study.

The third and final difficulty presented by Sommers' approach in that essay is her focus on composition-class composing—a focus on academic, belletristic, or literary writing that is shared by most other revision researchers, who have primarily examined the assigned writing of students, or writing by English teachers or professional essayists such as Donald Murray, or the writing of poetry and fiction, as in the *Paris Review* interviews edited by Malcolm Cowley (1958). In such academic and literary circumstances, writers in many cases may not have what Flower and Hayes (1980a, 1980b) have called *stored representations*—appropriate notions about purpose, audience, line of thought, or tone—when they begin to write. The student might say, vaguely, "I think I'll write about my summer vacation." The poet might say, "Hmmm . . . that windhover I saw this morning might make a good subject for a poem." Of course, the student would be much more likely to make such a self-conscious remark, since poets rarely have teachers give them assignments or ask them what they would like to write about this week. In any event, if we asked Baker or Franklin to write about their summer vacation or to write a sonnet, they might well display a decidedly nonlinear process of composing; but if their Firm's president asked them to develop a proposal for Company X, their composing process—in particular, their macroprocess—would probably be decidedly linear.

These objections to Sommers' illuminating essay would not be worth making were it not for the fact that, as theory trickles down to classroom practice, the distinction between recursive and linear models could lead teachers and students (and perhaps some researchers) to ignore the fact that linear as well as recursive *processes* or *strategies* are frequently employed in on-the-job situations. This fact does nothing to diminish the theoretical and practical usefulness of Flower and Hayes' recursiveness-oriented "cognitive process" model, for nothing in that model requires that writing cannot be rigidly staged. Naturally, based on their observation of student writers, Flower and Hayes have found little evidence of highly staged processes. In contrast, based on a single observation of one engineer writing in a business environment, Jack Selzer (1983) has found such evidence—and so have we in our study of two writers and eight proposals.

Consequently, although most previous studies have examined highly recursive writers, researchers and teachers would do a disservice to the Flower and Hayes model in assuming that highly staged writers do not exist, that a linear model fails to describe their processes, or that a linear model might be pedagogically useful. But our concern here is not to perpetuate a competition between linear and recursive models. From the perspective of our study, the recursive-oriented cognitive process model is clearly superior because it allows for both recursive and staged (linear) writing strategies or behaviors. It is no longer a case of choosing between the models; it is rather a case of recognizing different composing strategies, variant adaptations of a general model to different rhetorical situations.

Thus, the theoretical significance of our study is that Baker's and Franklin's composing strategies can be understood in terms of a cognitive process model that to date has mainly been used to describe and explain highly recursive strategies. In other words, while our approach is inherently stage-oriented (since it examines the writing process from a draft-by-draft perspective), it supports many claims made on behalf of the cognitive process model.

First, our documentation of the distinction between voluntary and nonvoluntary revisions supports Flower and Hayes' claim that networks of interactive goals (norms) are at work as writers revise, since many changes in idea require that writers develop new text-oriented goals that result in changes in cohesion, style, and usage.

In particular, our tracing of high-affect changes illustrates Flower and Hayes' idea that the existing text helps the writer make more precise his or her reader-based goals—at least to the extent that, as the idea takes shape in the first draft, it is consistently revised for reader impact in subsequent drafts.

Second, our detailed break-down of the proportions between rates of orientations and other variables in each revising session or draft (as shown in Appendix C.7 through C.14) illustrates and extends Flower and Hayes' idea of the simultaneity of different and even disparate goals (for example, thoroughness vs. conciseness). That is, Baker and Franklin do not, strictly speaking, stop generating text in order to review and revise existing text or to plan for new text; but in each stage or session of the composing process, whether generating or revising, they have their eyes on more than one goal or one aspect of the writing situation.

Third, by isolating and categorizing specific changes made in a given rhetorical context, our study has established a framework for documenting the specific factors involved as a writer reformulates a plan or goal. Our concepts of norms, orientations, and goals (in our much narrower sense of the word) may help to disinvolve several factors signified by Flower and Hayes' broad notion of "goals," which they range on a scale from abstract to specific. In contrast, we describe them in terms of the forces that motivate them (that is, the norms imposed by culture, by institutions, by genres, by readers and tasks, and by idiosyncrasy) and in terms of the elements of the rhetorical situation on which they act (that is, their orientations, which are divided into relatively more specific goals). Goals as we have defined them encourage a descending scale of specificity, leading us step-by-step from the most abstract formulation of a goal to its concrete embodiment in the text. "Signal the connection with a cohesive tie" becomes the more specific "signal the temporal relationship with a free modifier," which in turn becomes the yet more specific "insert the word 'later' here as a free adverbial modifier."

In sum, our study does nothing to deny the claim that a recursive model—or at least a cognitive process model which allows for recursiveness—is better than a linear model. But it appears to offer clear evidence that much nonacademic, nonbelletristic composing is highly staged. Based on our informal observations of a wide range of writers in the Firm, and also on our classroom observations of writers who wish to work for such companies, we believe that as writers become more skilled and more efficient in at least some kinds of on-the-job writing, they become more highly staged.

The pedagogical implication of such frequent staging in on-the-job writing is not that, in our teaching of composing skills, we should ignore the processes, subprocesses, goal setting, and other behaviors that Flower and Hayes have shown to be of great potential value. Rather, the prevalence of staging in two successful real-world writers implies that, at least in advanced composition classes (including business, technical, and scientific writing classes), we might well help students learn the skills and routines used by many successful writers in job situations.

Despite the limitations of our approach noted earlier, the variables of composition appear to offer a fruitful perspective for composition pedagogy. By focusing on purpose and motive as outlined in the norms, orientations, and goals, students can become aware of the complexities of revision within a clearcut frame of reference. Students may apply the variables to the analysis of documents and may also use them as guidelines for inventing, organizing, generating, and revising compositions—especially writing assignments based on a case approach, in which students are given a writing task to perform within the limits of a clearly described rhetorical situation involving an audience with specific characteristics relevant to the document to be composed.

At the same time, however, even when students and other writers can identify and anticipate their own and their readers' expectations and motives, they must still be able to shape a text appropriately in response to those insights. Having a method and a strategy is one thing; implementing them is quite another. For this latter task, our approach offers a framework of descending specificity, linking abstract concepts and operations with their concrete embodiment in texts. In this respect, we can draw particular conclusions about pedagogy from the differences between Baker and Franklin: both are experienced and highly skilled at determining their readers' needs and desires, but Baker, in our opinion, does a better job of adapting his prose accordingly because he has a greater "vocabulary" of linguistic and rhetorical strategies. Thus, from our perspective at least, our study of Baker, Franklin, and their management-consulting firm leads us to a renewed sense of the need for a well-rounded pedagogy for composition at all levels and for all varieties of writers—a pedagogy that achieves a balanced approach to the interrelated demands of the writing process, the written product, and language itself.

Appendixes
References

Appendix A: The Variables of Revision

1. The First Six Variables of Revision

Impetus: Is the change voluntary or nonvoluntary?
  Voluntary
  Nonvoluntary
    Involuntary (required by a voluntary change)
    Typographic (required by a typist's error)
    Second-Author (made by another writer or editor)

Item: What is changed?
  Chapter
  First-level heading group
  Second-level heading group
  Third-level heading group
  Paragraph group
  Paragraph
  Sentence group
  Sentence
  T-unit
  Macrosyntactic structure
  Phrase
  Word
  Alphanumeric character, affix, or other subword
  Punctuation mark

Process: How is the change made?
  Insert
  Delete

Replace
Join
Split
Move

Norm: What prompts the change?
Culture: The writer's background and training
Institution: The writer's environment at work
Genre: The format and other conventions of a genre
Personality: The writer's unique characteristics
Situation: The task and audience

Affective Impact: Is the affective impact low or high?
Low impact: Emotionally neutral for the audience
High impact: Emotionally pleasant or unpleasant for the audience

Orientation: What is the rhetorical focus?
Idea: The information and line of thought
Cohesion: The signals of relationships between ideas
Style: The configurations of linguistic and rhetorical elements
Usage: Sociolinguistic conventions (as in handbooks)

2. Errors of Cohesion (By Goal)

Goal 6: To signal relationships with a cohesive tie.
False coordination (usually misuse of "and")
Lack of cohesive tie
Lack of or misuse of article
Telegraphic style (lack of signal words)
Unclear or ambiguous pronoun reference
Unmarked relative clause (no relative pronoun)

Goal 7: To signal relationships with punctuation.
Comma splice (separation of two independent clauses with a comma)
Comma split (separation of subject and main verb with a comma)
Failure to punctuate the last element of a series
False parallel punctuation

Fused or run-on clause (unpunctuated added clause)
Lack of hyphen
Lack of or misplacement of apostrophe
Mispunctuation of a bound (restrictive) modifier
Misuse of semicolon to set off a free modifier
Nonparallel punctuation
Overpunctuation (other than comma split or set-off bound modifier)
Unpunctuated coordinate clause
Unpunctuated free modifier (for example, subordinate clause, appositive)

Goal 8: To signal relationships by graphic means.
Lack of heading
Nonparallel linguistic form for heading
Nonparallel typographic format for heading

Goal 9: To signal relationships through syntax.
Confusing sentence fragment
False grammatical subordination (misuse of free modifiers)
False parallelism of bound structures
False parallelism of free structures
False parallelism of independent clauses
Lack of desirable parallelism between free modifiers
Lack of desirable parallelism between independent clauses
Lack of echoing structures (failure to use parallelism)
Lack of given or new order
Lack of grammatical subordination (failure to use free modifiers)
Lack of required parallelism between bound structures
Shift between active and passive voice
Shift between direct and indirect discourse
Shift between major-form and minor-form sentence structures
Shift in grammatical mood
Shift in tense
Unclear reference for free modifier ("squinting modifier")

Goal 10: To signal relationships by lexical means.
Lack of backward reference (anaphoric cohesion)
Lack of forward reference (cataphoric cohesion)

Lack of or misuse of abbreviation
Lack of or misuse of acronym

3. Errors of Style (By Goal)

Goal 11: To be readable.
Awkward interruption of a structure with a free modifier
Hyperembedding of bound clauses (bound clause within bound clause)
Overloaded (overlong) structure (lack of segmentation)
Stacked nouns (hypernominalization; use of strings of modifier nouns)
Unnecessary anticipatory construction ("it is," "there are")
Unnecessary sentence frame ("Table 6 shows that . . .")

Goal 12: To condense.
Unnecessary passive voice
Unnecessary grammatical expletives ("We do use this")
Unnecessary nominalization (use of noun phrase rather than verb)

Goal 13: To avoid weak repetition.
Ineffective restatement (redundancy of clause or sentence)
Redundancy of word or phrase
Weak repetition (excessive or ineffective use of a word or phrase)

4. Errors of Usage (By Goal)

Goal 15: To spell correctly.
Inconsistent expression of numbers (numerals vs. words)
Misspelling
Misuse of homonym
Violation of a rule about expression of numbers (for example, "rule of ten")

Goal 16: To use idiomatic or conventional phrasing.
Inappropriate contraction

Inappropriate use of an abbreviation or acronym (for example, "Dear Prof.")
Nonidiomatic phrase

Goal 17: To capitalize letters correctly.
Misuse of lower-case letters
Misuse of upper-case letters

Goal 18: To observe usage.
Absurd dangling modifier
Inappropriate sentence fragment
Miscellaneous usage errors
Sexist language (especially pronouns)
Split infinitive
Use of banned personal pronoun
Use of banned word or phrase (for example, "is when")
Use of coordinator "And" at the beginning of a sentence
Use of demonstrative pronoun without a noun ("This is common")
Use of preposition at the end of a clause

Goal 19: To punctuate conventionally.
Failure to punctuate the last element in a series (when not confusing)
Lack of or misuse of nonsyntactic punctuation (for example, "Mr Brown")
Use of a colon in the middle of a structure
Use of a dash to set off an initial-position free modifier

Goal 20: To achieve grammatical agreement.
Double negative
Garbled syntax
Lack of article/noun agreement (for example, "a successful conclusions")
Lack of noun/noun agreement
Lack of noun/pronoun agreement
Lack of noun/verb agreement
Lack of pronoun/pronoun agreement
Wrong grammatical form of a word

5. The Goals of Composition

Idea

Goal 1: To be accurate. Removes or replaces inaccurate information or language (including jargon).

Goal 2: To be safe. Adds a qualifier; removes or replaces questionable claims or implications.

Goal 3: To be thorough. Develops an idea for logical or rhetorical consistency, for organizational or personal standards, or for situational needs.

Goal 4: To be relevant. Removes or replaces unneeded information.

Goal 5: To be coherent. Alters the logical or rhetorical structure of the text.

Cohesion

Goal 6: To signal relationships with a cohesive tie. For example, adverb, prepositional phrase, infinitive phrase, whether free or bound.

Goal 7: To signal relationships with punctuation.

Goal 8: To signal relationships by graphic means. For example, headings, white space, paragraph indentation, highlighting.

Goal 9: To signal relationships through syntax. For example, given/new order, parallelism, coordination, subordination.

Goal 10: To signal relationships by lexical means. For example, repetition of a key term in original or altered form, use of a synonym.

Style

Goal 11: To be readable. Recasts idea into more easily comprehensible structures through segmentation, desegmentation, or other rearrangement.

Goal 12: To condense. Eliminates wordiness.

Goal 13: To avoid weak repetition.

Goal 14: To sound good. Creates euphony or rhythm.

Usage

Goal 15: To spell correctly.
Goal 16: To use idiomatic or conventional phrasing.
Goal 17: To capitalize letters correctly.
Goal 18: To observe usage. For example, split infinitives, dangling modifiers.
Goal 19: To punctuate correctly.
Goal 20: To achieve grammatical agreement. For example, noun/verb, noun/noun, noun/pronoun, pronoun/pronoun, or conventional syntax.

High Affect

Goal 21: To avoid a threat. Removes or de-emphasizes a claim or implication that threatens the position or well-being of the reader.
Goal 22: To avoid an insult. Removes or de-emphasizes an offensive claim or implication.
Goal 23: To bond with the reader. Establishes rapport between reader and writer.
Goal 24: To build credit. Adds positive claims or implications about the writer's (or firm's) attributes or position; also avoids negative claims and implications.
Goal 25: To feed a wish. Adds claims or implications that stress positive results for the reader or that create or satisfy a need in the reader.
Goal 26: To stroke the reader. Adds claims or implications that commend or flatter the reader.

Appendix B: Sentence Structures

1. Macrosyntactic Structures

Independent Clauses

010 Base clause
Jim opened the door.
020 Coordinate clause
Jim opened the door, *and then he closed it.*
030 Added clause
Jim opened the door; *Louise shut it.*
040 Repeating clause
Jim succeeded in his task: *he opened the door.*
050 Inserted clause
Jim (*he hated a stuffy room*) opened the door.

Free Modifiers

110 -*ing* verb cluster (present participial phrase)
Feeling claustrophobic, Jim opened the door.
120 -*ed/-en* verb cluster (past participial phrase)
Startled by noise, Jim opened the door.
130 Infinitive verb cluster
To air the room, Jim opened the door.
140 "As is" verb cluster
As is clear, Jim opened the door.
150 Detached verb cluster
Jim opened the door, *and was glad he did.*

210 Noun cluster (appositive)
A *burglar of great skill*, Jim opened the door.
220 List cluster
Jim opened three things: *the door, a window, and a bottle.*
230 "Such as" cluster
Jim likes to open lots of things, *such as doors.*
310 Adjective cluster
Curious about the noise, Jim opened the door.
410 Adverb cluster
Slowly and carefully, Jim opened the door. (Developmental)
However, Jim opened the door. (Cohesive)
510 Free prepositional phrase
Like a butler, Jim opened the door. (Developmental)
As a result, Jim opened the door. (Cohesive)
610 Free subordinate clause (Non-restrictive)
Since the room was stuffy, Jim opened the door.
620 Free relative clause (Non-restrictive)
Jim opened the door, *which had blown shut.*
630 Free absolute clause (Non-restrictive)
His fingers trembling, Jim opened the door.
640 Quote- or thought-attributing clause
"I opened the door," *said Jim.*
Jim, *we now believe*, opened the door.

2. Internal Structures of Independent Clauses

Anticipatory construction ("It is")
    It is interesting that he opened the door.
Anticipatory construction ("There is")
    There is a door that he opened.
Elided construction (sentence fragment)
    A door to be opened.
Formulaic expression
    a = b.
Imperative
    Open the door.
Interrogative
    Did he open the door?

Was the door opened?
Inverted
  Opened he the door.
  Opened was the door.
Passive Voice
  The door was opened by him.
Passive + infinitive
  The door was opened to let in air.
Noun + copulative verb + infintive
  The door seemed to open.
Noun + copulative verb + noun or adjective
  The door became an obstacle.
  The door became open.
Noun + linking verb + adjective + noun
  The door-opening was worth it.
Noun + linking verb + phrase
  The door-opening activity was as follows.
Noun + linking verb + adjective
  The door was open.
Noun + linking verb + adjective + infinitive
  The door was likely to be open.
Noun + linking verb + infinitive
  The door was to be opened.
Noun + linking verb + noun
  The door was an antique.
Noun + linking verb + prepositional phrase
  The door was in the south wall.
Noun + linking verb + relative clause (with relative pronoun)
  We knew that he opened the door.
  The point is that he opened the door.
Noun + linking verb + relative clause (without relative pronoun)
  We knew he opened the door.
  The point is he opened the door.
Noun + linking verb + subordinate clause
  The opening of the door was because he needed air.
Noun + verb
  He chuckled.
Noun + verb + absolute
  He opened the door built into the wall.

Noun + verb + infinitive
  He wanted to open the door.
Noun + verb + noun
  He opened the door.
Noun + verb + noun + adjective
  He painted the door brown.
Noun + verb + noun + infinitive (result)
  He caused the door to open.
Noun + verb + noun + infinitive (purpose)
  He opened the door to go outside.
Noun + verb + noun + noun
  He considered the door an antique.
Noun + verb + relative clause (with relative pronoun)
  He thought that the door was open.
Noun + verb + relative clause (without relative pronoun)
  He thought the door was open.
Relative clause + verb
  That the door was opened seems clear.

Appendix C: Statistical Analyses of Composing/Revising Processes

1. Stylistic Variables: Four-Proposal Means of Rates and Percentages (By Author)

	Baker's Four Proposals		Franklin's Four Proposals	
	Mean	S.D.	Mean	S.D.
Complexity and Variability				
Words per T-unit*	19.7	0.6	21.9	0.9
Words per independent clause	14.7	0.2	17.9	1.3
S.D. of T-unit mean	14.9	3.2	11.5	0.9
T-unit/Ind-clause difference	5.0	0.6	4.1	1.2
Bound clauses per 100 T-units	30	5.7	43	10.5
Total words in largest T-unit	138	57	73	7
Variety				
Kinds of macro structures	16	1.5	12	1.2
Initial-position FMs (Pct)	20	2.2	19	4.8
Middle-position FMs (Pct)	6	1.6	12	5.6
Final-position FMs (Pct)	17	2.9	8	3.1
Words in final-pos FMs (Pct)	16	2.8	7	3.6
FMs inside other FMs (Pct)	7	2.1	3	3.3
Number of clause types	22	1.2	17	1.7
Linguistic Cohesion				
Cohesive ties per 100 T-units*	45	3.1	42	21.9
Cohesive FMs per 100 T-units	16	2.3	18	5.6
Pronouns per 100 T-units	132	5.9	172	17.7
Echoes per 100 T-units	14	3.5	9	4.7

	Baker's Four Proposals		Franklin's Four Proposals	
	Mean	S.D.	Mean	S.D.
Non-comma punctuation (Pct)	22	7.0	29	7.6
Unpunctuated structures (Pct)	3	2.4	15	3.9
Cohesion errors per 100 T-units	15	3.4	15	5.3
Graphic Cohesion				
Headings per 100 T-units*	14	8.7	21	5.0
Highlights per 100 T-units	19	7.0	27	11.4
Italics per 100 T-units	6	3.7	2	3.9
Words per paragraph*	60	15.2	53	1.7
S.D. of paragraph mean	40	10.8	29	3.9
Style				
Passive-voice clauses (Pct)	12	5.2	21	6.8
Anticipatory clauses (Pct)	4	1.3	5	4.4
Framed claues (Pct)	5	2.1	17	3.8
Total weak clauses (Pct)*	20	3.9	42	6.4
Personal pronouns per 100 T-units	51	8.2	49	7.1
Style errors per 100 T-units	3	1.5	10	4.0
Usage				
Usage errors per 100 T-units	18	3.0	24	4.3
Mispunctuated structures (Pct)	4	1.5	7	2.4

Note: As explained in chapter 2, rates in this and all subsequent tables are expressed per 100 T-units for the item named. Items marked with an asterisk are included in draft-by-draft comparisons in 4.7 through 4.14 (Appendix C).

2. Stylistic Variables (By Proposal)

	Bak A	Bak B	Bak C	Bak D	Fra A	Fra B	Fra C	Fra D
Complexity and Variability								
Words per T-unit (mean)*	19.4	19.9	18.9	20.4	20.9	22.3	21.4	23.0
Words per ind clause*	14.8	14.8	14.4	14.6	17.9	19.5	16.4	17.7
S.D. of T-unit mean	16.2	10.7	14.4	18.2	12.5	11.0	11.9	10.5
T-unit/IC difference	4.6	5.0	4.5	5.8	3.1	2.9	5.0	5.2
Bound clauses rate	27	24	34	26	27	48	47	49
Words in largest T-unit	175	72	110	194	78	80	64	70

	Bak A	Bak B	Bak C	Bak D	Fra A	Fra B	Fra C	Fra D
Variety								
Kinds of macro structures	17	17	14	15	11	11	13	13
Initial-position FMs (Pct)	22	20	21	17	23	18	22	12
Middle-position FMs (Pct)	6	4	6	8	6	16	8	17
Final-position FMs (Pct)	14	15	20	19	6	4	9	11
Words in fin-pos FMs (Pct)*	14	14	16	20	5	4	12	7
FMs inside other FMs (Pct)	7	4	9	7	3	0	0	7
Number of clause types	23	21	21	23	17	16	15	19
Linguistic Cohesion								
Cohesive ties rate	48	47	45	41	26	73	42	26
Cohesive FMs rate	18	14	18	14	17	26	16	13
Pronouns rate	130	125	139	134	149	186	168	186
Echoes rate	16	10	11	17	4	15	7	8
Non-comma punctuation (Pct)	14	25	19	30	29	32	19	37
Unpunctuated structures (Pct)	6	0	3	3	9	16	18	15
Cohesion errors rate	17	10	18	14	12	22	10	16
Graphic Cohesion								
Headings rate	20	22	5	7	18	28	21	17
Highlights rate	17	16	13	29	40	13	31	24
Italics rate	6	10	1	6	0	0	8	1
Words/paragraph	49	52	82	55	55	51	54	53
S.D. of paragraph mean	29	33	53	43	29	24	31	33
Style								
Passive-voice clauses (Pct)	18	14	6	10	11	21	26	25
Anticipatory clauses (Pct)	3	2	5	4	10	6	2	0
Framed clauses (Pct)	5	2	7	5	14	16	22	14
Total weak clauses (Pct)	26	18	18	19	35	43	50	39
Personal pronouns (Pct)	44	63	49	49	50	41	47	58
Style errors rate	2	4	5	2	4	12	10	13
Usage								
Usage errors rate	19	22	15	17	22	20	24	30
Mispunctuated structures (Pct)	5	3	6	3	5	9	4	8

Note: As explained in chapter 2, rates in this and all subsequent tables are expressed per 100 T-units for the item named. Items marked with an asterisk are included in draft-by-draft comparisons in 4.7 through 4.14 (Appendix C).

3. Overview of Voluntary Revisions: Norms, Processes, and Orientations (In Percents, by Author)

	Baker's Four Proposals		Franklin's Four Proposals	
	Mean	S.D.	Mean	S.D.
Impetus				
Voluntary*	74	4.9	86	3.8
(Non-Voluntary)*	(26)	(4.9)	(14)	(3.8)
(Involuntary)	(15)	(1.3)	(10)	(3.2)
(Typographic)	(6)	(2.9)	(4)	(3.6)
(Second-Author)	(5)	(5.9)	(0)	(0.0)
Norm				
Cultural	80	9.6	83	11.6
Situational	18	7.0	17	11.1
Generic	1	1.4	0	0.0
Institutional	1	0.8	1	0.5
Personal	1	0.8	1	0.5
Process				
Insert	37	3.6	29	11.1
Delete	15	1.3	13	5.9
Replace	36	5.1	52	8.7
Split	6	2.4	3	1.3
Join	3	0.5	2	1.5
Move	4	2.0	2	1.5
Pct over sentence*	5	2.2	3	0.6
Orientation/High Affect				
High affect*	17	7.3	12	6.1
Idea*	33	5.0	44	4.7
Cohesion*	22	3.3	16	3.1
Style*	22	1.7	23	7.3
Usage*	7	2.0	5	2.1

4. Overview of Voluntary Revisions: Norms, Processes, and Orientations (In Percents, by Proposal)

	Bak A	Bak B	Bak C	Bak D	Fra A	Fra B	Fra C	Fra D
Impetus								
Voluntary	76	77	77	67	91	83	87	83
(Non-Voluntary)	(24)	(23)	(23)	(33)	(9)	(17)	(13)	(17)
(Involuntary)	(14)	(16)	(15)	(13)	(7)	(13)	(12)	(7)
(Typographic)	(2)	(7)	(8)	(8)	(2)	(5)	(1)	(9)
(Second-Author)	(7)	(0)	(0)	(12)	(0)	(0)	(0)	(0)
Norm								
Cultural	66	85	82	87	84	67	94	88
Situational	27	14	18	11	16	32	6	12
Generic	3	0	0	1	0	0	0	0
Institutional	2	1	0	1	0	1	0	0
Personal	2	1	0	1	1	0	0	0
Process								
Insert	32	39	36	40	39	15	37	26
Delete	17	14	15	15	8	19	16	7
Replace	42	37	34	30	48	60	41	57
Split	4	4	9	5	2	3	3	5
Join	2	3	2	3	1	2	1	5
Move	3	3	3	7	3	1	3	0
Pct over sentence	5	4	3	8	3	2	2	3
Orientation/High Affect								
High affect	27	12	18	11	15	18	4	11
Idea	28	32	33	40	51	43	43	40
Cohesion	17	24	21	24	18	11	16	17
Style	23	22	22	19	13	23	29	28
Usage	6	10	6	6	3	5	8	5

5. Overview of Voluntary Revisions: Goals
(In Percents, by Author)

	Baker's Four Proposals		Franklin's Four Proposals	
	Mean	S.D.	Mean	S.D.
Idea				
1 Be accurate	20	4.8	32	2.9
2 Be safe	2	0.8	3	1.0
3 Be thorough	7	2.8	9	5.6
4 Be relevant	2	0.8	2	2.4
5 Be coherent	4	2.4	1	1.5
Cohesion				
6 Signal with cohesive tie	5	2.4	6	1.3
7 Signal with punctuation	3	1.3	1	1.3
8 Signal with graphics	5	2.5	2	2.4
9 Signal with syntax	4	2.3	1	0.5
10 Signal with reference	5	1.5	5	1.8
Style				
11 Segment	6	2.9	4	3.7
12 Be concise	11	3.1	16	5.7
13 Avoid weak repetition	2	1.5	2	1.0
14 Sound better	2	0.8	1	1.5
Usage				
15 Spell correctly	0	0.0	0	0.0
16 Improve idiom or phrasing	2	1.0	4	1.7
17 Capitalize correctly	2	1.0	1	1.0
18 Observe usage	1	0.6	0	0.0
19 Punctuate conventionally	2	1.0	0	0.0
20 Achieve agreement	2	0.6	1	1.0
High Affect				
21 Avoid threat	3	3.0	1	1.0
22 Avoid insult	1	2.0	2	1.3
23 Bond with audience	1	0.0	1	1.2
24 Build credit	6	2.4	3	2.1
25 Feed a wish	6	3.1	6	3.9
26 Stroke the audience	2	2.4	1	0.6

6. Overview of Voluntary Revisions: Goals
(In Percents, by Proposal)

	Bak A	Bak B	Bak C	Bak D	Fra A	Fra B	Fra C	Fra D
Idea								
1 Be accurate	14	18	25	22	31	34	28	34
2 Be safe	2	3	1	2	3	1	3	3
3 Be thorough	9	9	3	7	16	4	11	5
4 Be relevant	2	2	1	3	2	5	0	0
5 Be coherent	2	2	3	7	0	0	3	0
Cohesion								
6 Signal with cohesive tie	2	5	8	5	4	6	5	7
7 Signal with punctuation	2	3	3	5	0	1	1	3
8 Signal with graphics	4	2	4	8	5	0	0	2
9 Signal with syntax	5	7	1	2	2	1	1	1
10 Signal with reference	4	7	4	4	6	3	7	4
Style								
11 Segment text	3	5	10	6	0	4	3	9
12 Be concise	14	13	11	7	9	16	23	17
13 Avoid weak repetition	3	1	1	4	1	3	3	2
14 Sound better	3	2	1	2	3	0	0	0
Usage								
15 Spell correctly	0	0	0	0	0	0	0	0
16 Improve idiom or phrasing	3	3	2	1	3	2	6	3
17 Capitalize correctly	1	3	1	1	0	2	0	1
18 Observe usage	1	1	0	0	0	0	0	0
19 Punctuate conventionally	1	3	1	1	0	0	0	0
20 Achieve agreement	1	1	2	2	0	1	2	0
High Affect (Mainly Idea)								
21 Avoid a threat	7	1	1	1	0	2	0	1
22 Avoid an insult	4	0	0	0	2	1	3	0
23 Bond with audience	1	1	1	1	2	2	0	0
24 Build credit	8	8	3	6	2	5	1	5
25 Feed a wish	7	2	9	4	9	9	1	4
26 Stroke the audience	1	0	5	0	1	0	0	1

7. Summary of Revisions to Bak-A (By Draft and Part)

	1	2a	2b	3	4	Tot
Problem Section						
Voluntary	——	94	155	140	(0)	389
Rate over sentence	——	10	6	3	(0)	19
High affect	——	34	33	65	(0)	132
Idea	——	9	30	35	(0)	74
Cohesion	——	20	12	16	(9)	48
Style	——	24	77	18	(6)	119
Usage	——	7	4	6	(14)	18
(Nonvol usage)	——	(1)	(14)	(11)	(4)	(26)
T-unit mean	18.0	17.8	15.7	18.1	18.2	——
Ind clause mean	16.4	15.6	13.6	14.9	14.8	——
Fin-pos FM words	1	3	3	9	10	——
Cohesive ties rate	41	48	48	49	49	——
Headings rate	1	4	5	6	6	——
Paragraph mean	57	53	42	45	45	——
Pct weak clauses	21	19	18	17	17	——
Usage error rate	26	20	19	24	19	——
Method Section						
Voluntary	——	——	119	147	(15)	266
Rate over sentence	——	——	5	11	(0)	16
High affect	——	——	17	23	(3)	40
Idea	——	——	46	71	(10)	117
Cohesion	——	——	24	35	(2)	59
Style	——	——	15	15	(0)	30
Usage	——	——	17	3	(0)	20
(Nonvol usage)	——	——	(12)	(4)	(0)	(16)
T-unit mean	——	19.6	20.8	20.1	20.1	——
Ind clause mean	——	13.5	13.6	13.9	13.9	——
Fin-pos FM words	——	18	25	20	20	——
Cohesive ties rate	——	58	56	57	57	——
Headings rate	——	41	40	43	43	——
Paragraph mean	——	48	49	44	45	——
Pct weak clauses	——	29	29	31	32	——
Usage error rate	——	25	15	18	17	——
Implementation Section						
Voluntary	——	——	96	54	(54)	150
Rate over sentence	——	——	4	4	(0)	8

	1	2a	2b	3	4	Tot
High affect	——	——	27	28	(15)	55
Idea	——	——	23	20	(12)	43
Cohesion	——	——	23	12	(3)	35
Style	——	——	19	0	(9)	19
Usage	——	——	4	4	(15)	8
(Nonvol usage)	——	——	(12)	(8)	(15)	(20)
T-unit mean	——	20.0	20.6	19.8	20.1	——
Ind clause mean	——	14.0	14.9	16.4	16.7	——
Fin-pos FM words	——	21	19	10	9	——
Cohesive ties rate	——	46	36	33	25	——
Headings rate	——	12	12	10	9	——
Paragraph mean	——	65	57	60	58	——
Pct weak clauses	——	23	24	23	25	——
Usage error rate	——	39	24	23	25	——

8. Summary of Revisions to Bak-B (By Draft and Part)

	1	2	3	4	Tot
Problem Section					
Voluntary	——	304	182	21	507
Rate over sentence	——	13	13	0	26
High affect	——	26	48	3	77
Idea	——	143	43	6	192
Cohesion	——	39	30	6	75
Style	——	83	13	0	96
Usage	——	13	48	6	67
(Nonvol usage)	——	(35)	(26)	(9)	(70)
T-unit mean	25.7	28.3	24.7	24.8	——
Ind clause mean	17.3	17.7	15.1	14.8	——
Fin-pos FM words	18	23	22	24	——
Cohesive ties rate	57	52	44	44	——
Headings rate	35	39	30	30	——
Paragraph mean	42	43	44	44	——
Pct weak clauses	35	30	30	30	——
Usage error rate	70	48	41	41	——
Method Section					
Voluntary	——	186	34	8	228
Rate over sentence	——	5	2	0	7

	1	2	3	4	Tot
High affect	——	8	2	0	10
Idea	——	48	19	3	70
Cohesion	——	74	5	1	80
Style	——	48	6	0	54
Usage	——	8	2	4	14
(Nonvol usage)	——	(32)	(0)	(11)	(43)
T-unit mean	21.3	19.4	19.3	19.3	——
Ind clause mean	16.4	15.0	14.5	14.5	——
Fin-pos FM words	12	12	14	14	——
Cohesive ties rate	60	55	53	53	——
Headings rate	32	25	23	23	——
Paragraph mean	51	61	62	62	——
Pct weak clauses	26	20	20	20	——
Usage error rate	31	11	13	13	——

Implementation Section

	1	2	3	4	Tot
Voluntary	——	——	116	27	143
Rate over sentence	——	——	2	3	5
High affect	——	——	31	0	31
Idea	——	——	29	8	37
Cohesion	——	——	24	5	29
Style	——	——	27	6	33
Usage	——	——	5	8	13
(Nonvol usage)	——	——	(4)	(11)	(15)
T-unit mean	——	18.3	18.3	18.3	——
Ind clause mean	——	15.7	15.5	15.4	——
Fin-pos FM words	——	7	8	9	——
Cohesive ties rate	——	39	40	41	——
Headings rate	——	16	19	19	——
Paragraph mean	——	47	47	47	——
Pct weak clauses	——	13	11	10	——
Usage error rate	——	29	31	25	——

9. Summary of Revisions to Bak-C (By Draft and Part)

	1	2	3	4	5	Tot
Problem Section						
Voluntary	——	120	92	42	9	263
Rate over sentence	——	0	4	4	0	8
High affect	——	20	23	8	0	51
Idea	——	68	35	15	0	118
Cohesion	——	4	15	15	3	37
Style	——	24	15	4	3	46
Usage	——	4	4	0	3	11
(Nonvol usage)	——	(24)	(12)	(12)	(0)	(48)
T-unit mean	18.2	18.0	15.8	17.9	17.8	——
Ind clause mean	11.5	10.9	11.1	11.4	11.4	——
Fin-pos FM words	28	30	22	29	29	——
Cohesive ties rate	48	42	48	55	55	——
Headings rate	4	4	4	3	3	——
Paragraph mean	65	67	71	70	69	——
Pct weak clauses	32	27	27	27	27	——
Usage error rate	24	19	22	23	23	——
Method Section						
Voluntary	——	77	66	32	20	195
Rate over sentence	——	4	0	0	2	6
High affect	——	15	16	2	4	37
Idea	——	15	20	8	6	49
Cohesion	——	22	14	6	6	48
Style	——	18	16	12	4	50
Usage	——	7	0	4	0	11
(Nonvol usage)	——	(16)	(16)	(8)	(4)	(44)
T-unit mean	20.8	20.6	19.3	19.0	19.5	——
Ind clause mean	17.3	16.5	16.1	15.9	15.9	——
Fin-pos FM words	7	10	11	11	11	——
Cohesive ties rate	46	41	39	39	41	——
Headings rate	4	6	8	8	8	——
Paragraph mean	96	88	91	90	100	——
Pct weak clauses	18	20	16	16	16	——
Usage error rate	16	14	14	14	12	——
Implementation Section						
Voluntary	——	——	——	31	16	47
Rate over sentence	——	——	——	0	0	0

	1	2	3	4	5	Tot
High affect	——	——	——	0	0	0
Idea	——	——	——	15	8	23
Cohesion	——	——	——	0	8	8
Style	——	——	——	8	0	8
Usage	——	——	——	8	0	8
(Nonvol usage)	——	——	——	(0)	(0)	(0)
T-unit mean	——	——	15.5	19.6	19.3	——
Ind clause mean	——	——	12.8	16.0	15.9	——
Fin-pos FM words	——	——	8	10	10	——
Cohesive ties rate	——	——	25	46	39	——
Headings rate	——	——	13	8	15	——
Paragraph mean	——	——	41	64	63	——
Pct weak clauses	——	——	13	8	8	——
Usage error rate	——	——	0	8	8	——

10. Summary of Revisions to Bak-D (By Draft and Part)

	1	2	3	Tot
Problem Section				
Voluntary	——	409	31	440
Rate over sentence	——	41	5	46
High affect	——	28	3	31
Idea	——	203	12	215
Cohesion	——	53	8	61
Style	——	97	8	105
Usage	——	28	0	28
(Nonvol usage)	——	(53)	(11)	(64)
T-unit mean	21.3	18.9	18.9	——
Ind clause mean	15.4	14.2	14.1	——
Fin-pos FM words	11	13	14	——
Cohesive ties rate	41	41	44	——
Headings rate	3	4	4	——
Paragraph mean	97	74	71	——
Pct weak clauses	13	23	23	——
Usage error rate	38	22	17	——
Method Section				
Voluntary	——	87	36	123
Rate over sentence	——	2	2	4

	1	2	3	Tot
High affect	——	12	7	19
Idea	——	25	16	41
Cohesion	——	35	4	39
Style	——	9	9	18
Usage	——	6	0	6
(Nonvol usage)	——	(18)	(9)	(27)
T-unit mean	19.8	21.1	21.7	——
Ind clause mean	14.0	14.2	14.5	——
Fin-pos FM words	21	24	25	——
Cohesive ties rate	37	39	41	——
Headings rate	9	12	11	——
Paragraph mean	49	50	50	——
Pct weak clauses	19	16	15	——
Usage error rate	32	18	21	——

Implementation Section

	1	2	3	Tot
Voluntary	——	——	(6)	(6)
Rate over sentence	——	——	(2)	(2)
High affect	——	——	(0)	(0)
Idea	——	——	(2)	(2)
Cohesion	——	——	(2)	(2)
Style	——	——	(0)	(0)
Usage	——	——	(2)	(2)
(Nonvol usage)	——	——	(13)	(13)
T-unit mean	——	19.4	19.8	——
Ind clause mean	——	15.6	15.8	——
Fin-pos FM words	——	14	15	——
Cohesive ties rate	——	34	36	——
Headings rate	——	6	6	——
Paragraph mean	——	46	49	——
Pct weak clauses	——	21	21	——
Usage error rate	——	13	11	——

11. Summary of Revisions to Fra-A (By Draft and Part)

	1	2	3	4	Tot
Problem Section					
Voluntary	——	114	53	25	192
Rate over sentence	——	0	7	0	7
High affect	——	0	0	6	6
Idea	——	80	20	12	113
Cohesion	——	20	20	6	46
Style	——	7	13	0	20
Usage	——	7	0	0	7
(Nonvol usage)	——	(7)	(7)	(0)	(14)
T-unit mean	18.5	19.7	18.5	18.2	——
Ind clause mean	16.9	17.9	16.1	15.9	——
Fin-pos FM words	5	4	4	4	——
Cohesive ties rate	27	27	19	18	——
Headings rate	20	20	19	18	——
Paragraph mean	56	59	49	52	——
Pct weak clauses	33	33	31	29	——
Usage error rate	0	0	0	12	——
Method Section					
Voluntary	——	143	43	62	248
Rate over sentence	——	0	0	0	0
High affect	——	21	0	18	39
Idea	——	82	21	29	132
Cohesion	——	11	18	11	40
Style	——	25	4	4	33
Usage	——	4	0	0	4
(Nonvol usage)	——	(0)	(4)	(4)	(8)
T-unit mean	25.1	25.1	25.1	23.0	——
Ind clause mean	20.8	20.8	20.7	19.1	——
Fin-pos FM words	2	2	2	8	——
Cohesive ties rate	21	21	21	26	——
Headings rate	21	21	21	20	——
Paragraph mean	70	70	70	73	——
Pct weak clauses	32	32	29	34	——
Usage error rate	36	39	39	29	——
Implementation Section					
Voluntary	——	81	——	5	86
Rate over sentence	——	5	——	5	10

	1	2	3	4	Tot
High affect	——	24	——	0	24
Idea	——	19	——	5	24
Cohesion	——	14	——	0	14
Style	——	14	——	0	14
Usage	——	10	——	0	10
(Nonvol usage)	——	(10)	——	(0)	(10)
T-unit mean	19.9	20.0	——	20.0	——
Ind clause mean	16.4	17.5	——	17.5	——
Fin-pos FM words	5	1	——	1	——
Cohesive ties rate	38	38	——	38	——
Headings rate	24	24	——	24	——
Paragraph mean	42	38	——	38	——
Pct weak clauses	43	38	——	38	——
Usage error rate	38	19	——	19	——

12. Summary of Revisions to Fra-B (By Draft and Part)

	1	2	3	Tot
Problem Section				
Voluntary	——	182	42	224
Rate over sentence	——	0	0	0
High affect	——	18	17	35
Idea	——	64	8	72
Cohesion	——	27	0	27
Style	——	73	17	90
Usage	——	0	0	0
(Nonvol usage)	——	(9)	(0)	(9)
T-unit mean	26.2	25.7	25.7	——
Ind clause mean	22.7	20.9	22.3	——
Fin-pos FM words	0	3	0	——
Cohesive ties rate	36	55	55	——
Headings rate	27	25	25	——
Paragraph mean	58	57	57	——
Pct weak clauses	45	42	42	——
Usage error rate	18	9	9	——
Method Section				
Voluntary	——	108	33	141
Rate over sentence	——	0	2	2

	1	2	3	Tot
High affect	——	18	7	25
Idea	——	56	13	69
Cohesion	——	11	4	15
Style	——	16	7	23
Usage	——	7	2	9
(Nonvol usage)	——	(2)	(9)	(11)
T-unit mean	20.9	21.8	22.0	——
Ind clause mean	18.4	19.0	18.9	——
Fin-pos FM words	5	5	6	——
Cohesive ties rate	96	87	89	——
Headings rate	36	35	35	——
Paragraph mean	47	49	49	——
Pct weak clauses	36	37	39	——
Usage error rate	20	29	22	——

Implementation Section

	1	2	3	Tot
Voluntary	——	117	27	144
Rate over sentence	——	9	0	9
High affect	——	36	0	36
Idea	——	45	9	54
Cohesion	——	0	9	9
Style	——	27	9	36
Usage	——	9	0	9
(Nonvol usage)	——	(18)	(9)	(27)
T-unit mean	23.5	20.2	20.6	——
Ind clause mean	21.5	18.3	18.7	——
Fin-pos FM words	0	0	0	——
Cohesive ties rate	36	31	31	——
Headings rate	27	23	23	——
Paragraph mean	52	53	54	——
Pct weak clauses	55	54	54	——
Usage error rate	27	23	23	——

13. Summary of Revisions to Fra-C (By Draft and Part)

	1	2	3	Tot
Problem Section				
Voluntary	——	150	88	238
Rate over sentence	——	0	0	0
High affect	——	6	12	18
Idea	——	72	18	90
Cohesion	——	22	29	51
Style	——	44	29	73
Usage	——	6	0	6
(Nonvol usage)	——	(11)	(6)	(17)
T-unit mean	21.1	22.3	22.4	——
Ind clause mean	17.3	17.1	17.0	——
Fin-pos FM words	4	10	10	——
Cohesive ties rate	33	41	41	——
Headings rate	17	18	18	——
Paragraph mean	63	63	63	——
Pct weak clauses	56	59	59	——
Usage error rate	28	18	18	——
Method Section				
Voluntary	——	178	61	239
Rate over sentence	——	4	0	4
High affect	——	4	0	4
Idea	——	65	35	100
Cohesion	——	26	9	35
Style	——	48	17	65
Usage	——	35	0	35
(Nonvol usage)	——	(17)	(9)	(26)
T-unit mean	26.3	25.9	29.4	——
Ind clause mean	17.9	18.6	18.8	——
Fin-pos FM words	24	22	22	——
Cohesive ties rate	78	75	81	——
Headings rate	43	39	39	——
Paragraph mean	47	48	62	——
Pct weak clauses	26	30	35	——
Usage error rate	44	38	48	——
Implementation Section				
Voluntary	——	36	20	56
Rate over sentence	——	3	0	3

	1	2	3	Tot
High affect	——	0	3	3
Idea	——	18	14	32
Cohesion	——	6	3	9
Style	——	12	0	12
Usage	——	0	0	0
(Nonvol usage)	——	(0)	(0)	(0)
T-unit mean	16.1	16.2	16.8	——
Ind clause mean	14.2	14.1	14.7	——
Fin-pos FM words	4	5	5	——
Cohesive ties rate	18	22	23	——
Headings rate	18	19	18	——
Paragraph mean	42	42	45	——
Pct weak clauses	50	47	45	——
Usage error rate	3	6	15	——

14. Summary of Revisions to Fra-D (By Draft and Part)

	1	2	3	Tot
Problem Section				
Voluntary	——	185	28	213
Rate over sentence	——	5	0	5
High affect	——	28	0	28
Idea	——	85	7	92
Cohesion	——	23	12	35
Style	——	44	7	51
Usage	——	5	2	7
(Nonvol usage)	——	(10)	(5)	(15)
T-unit mean	23.0	22.1	23.0	——
Ind clause mean	17.3	17.2	17.0	——
Fin-pos FM words	12	10	11	——
Cohesive ties rate	21	24	29	——
Headings rate	8	7	7	——
Paragraph mean	58	50	52	——
Pct weak clauses	38	37	37	——
Usage error rate	32	24	24	——
Method Section				
Voluntary	——	181	43	224
Rate over sentence	——	8	0	8

	1	2	3	Tot
High affect	——	17	0	17
Idea	——	50	19	69
Cohesion	——	38	5	43
Style	——	63	14	77
Usage	——	13	5	18
(Nonvol usage)	——	(8)	(19)	(27)
T-unit mean	22.1	22.5	23.0	——
Ind clause mean	15.7	19.1	18.9	——
Fin-pos FM words	9	3	3	——
Cohesive ties rate	29	27	27	——
Headings rate	33	38	38	——
Paragraph mean	66	55	56	——
Pct weak clauses	33	38	38	——
Usage error rate	63	50	46	——
Implementation Section				
Voluntary	——	115	71	186
Rate over sentence	——	14	0	14
High affect	——	0	14	14
Idea	——	57	43	100
Cohesion	——	29	0	29
Style	——	29	14	43
Usage	——	0	0	0
(Nonvol usage)	——	(0)	(14)	(14)
T-unit mean	16.9	17.3	23.0	——
Ind clause mean	15.7	16.3	18.9	——
Fin-pos FM words	0	0	0	——
Cohesive ties rate	14	14	0	——
Headings rate	43	43	43	——
Paragraph mean	30	40	46	——
Pct weak clauses	57	14	17	——
Usage error rate	86	43	83	——

References

Allen, Donald, and Rebecca Guy. 1978. *Conversation analysis: The sociology of talk*. Janua Linguarum, Series Minor, no. 200. The Hague: Mouton.

Austin, J. L. 1975. *How to do things with words*. 2nd ed. William James Lecture Series. Cambridge, MA: Harvard Univ. Pr.

Baugh, Albert C. 1957. *A history of the English language*. 2nd ed. New York: Appleton-Century-Crofts.

Beuhler, Mary Fran. 1977. Controlled flexibility in technical editing: The levels-of-edit concept at JPL. *Technical Communication* 24 (First Quarter): 1–4.

Bridwell, Lillian. 1980. Revising strategies in twelfth grade students' transactional writing. *Research in the Teaching of English* 14 (October): 197–222.

Broadhead, Glenn J, and James A. Berlin. 1982. Teaching and measuring sentence skills: The importance of length, variability, variety, and punctuation. Educational Resources Information Center Report, ED 208 409 (March 1982).

Broadhead, Glenn J, James A. Berlin, and Marlis M. Broadhead. 1982. Sentence structure in academic prose and its implications for college writing teachers. *Research in the Teaching of English* 16 (October): 225–40.

Broadhead, Glenn J, and Richard C. Freed. Analyzing the Faigley-Witte taxonomy. Forthcoming. *College Composition and Communication*.

Christensen, Francis, and Bonnijean Christensen. 1978. *Notes toward a new rhetoric*. 2nd ed. New York: Harper and Row.

Cowley, Malcolm (Ed.). 1958. *Writers at work: The Paris Review interviews*, vol. 1. New York: Viking Press.

Crothers, Edward J. 1979. *Paragraph structure inference*. Norwood, NJ: Ablex.

Dijk, Teun van. 1980. *Macrostructures: An interdisciplinary study of global structures in discourse, interaction, and cognition*. Hillsdale, NJ: Lawrence Erlbaum.

Emig, Janet. 1971. *The composing processes of twelfth graders*. NCTE Research Report, No. 13. Urbana, IL: National Council of Teachers of English.

Faigley, Lester, and Stephen Witte. 1981. Analyzing revision. *College Composition and Communication* 4 (December): 400–414.

Flesch, Rudolf. 1951. *How to test readability*. New York: Harper and Brothers.

Flower, Linda, and John R. Hayes. 1980a. The cognition of discovery: Defining a rhetorical problem. *College Composition and Communication* 31 (February): 21–32.

———. 1980b. Identifying the organization of writing processes. In *Cognitive processes in writing*, ed. Lee Gregg and Erwin Steinberg, 3–30. Hillsdale, NJ: Lawrence Erlbaum.

———. 1981. A cognitive process theory of writing. *College Composition and Communication* 32 (December): 365–87.

Grice, H. P. 1975. Logic and conversation. In *Syntax and semantics 3: Speech acts*, ed. Peter Cole and J. L. Morgan, 41–58. New York: Academic Press.

Halliday, Michael A. K. 1967, 1968. Notes on transitivity and theme in English. Parts 1–3. Journal of Linguistics 3:37–81, 199–244; 4: 179–215.

Halliday, Michael A. K., and Ruqaiya Hasan. 1976. *Cohesion in English*. London: Longman.

Hunt, Kellogg. 1966. Recent measures in syntactic development. *Elementary English* 43 (November): 732–39.

Langer, Judith A. 1984. Musings. *Research in the Teaching of English* 18 (May): 117–18.

Mathes, J. C., and Dwight W. Stevenson. 1976. *Designing technical reports: Writing for audiences in organizations*. Indianapolis: Bobbs-Merrill.

Matsuhashi, Ann. 1981. Pausing and planning: The tempo of written discourse production. *Research in the Teaching of English* 15 (May): 113–34.

Morenberg, Max, Donald Daiker, and Andrew Kerek. 1978. Sentence combining at the college level: An experimental study. *Research in the Teaching of English* 12(3): 245–56.

Murray, Donald. 1978. Internal revision: A process of discovery. In *Research on composing: Points of departure*, ed. Charles Cooper and Lee Odell, 85–103. Urbana, IL: National Council of Teachers of English.

Odell, Lee, and Dixie Goswami. 1982. Writing in a non-academic setting. *Research in the Teaching of English* 16 (October): 201–23.

Perl, Sondra. 1979. The composing processes of unskilled college writers. *Research in the Teaching of English* 13 (December): 317–36.

Searle, John R. 1969. *Speech acts: An essay in the philosophy of language*. Cambridge: Cambridge Univ. Pr.

Selzer, Jack. 1983. The composing processes of an engineer. *College Composition and Communication* 34 (May): 178–87.

Sommers, Nancy. 1980. Revision strategies of student writers and experienced adult writers. *College Composition and Communication* 31 (December): 378–88.

Williams, Joseph M. 1977. Linguistic responsibility. *College Composition and Communication* 39 (September): 8–17.

Witte, Stephen P. 1983. Topical structure and revision: An exploratory study. *College Composition and Communication* 34 (October): 313–48.

Glenn J   essors of
English   graduate
and grad   nication.
Both hav   usiness.

Broad   ialifornia
at Davis   composition ped

Freed   tate, received h   . He has
publishe   ell as on
Hawthoi